A WEALTH OF PRACTICAL, INSIGHTFUL INFORMATION
FOR ANYONE WHO WANTS GREATER SELF-ESTEEM

- Inspiring stories from the author's own experiences
- Simple self-help exercises you can do alone or with family and friends
- One-on-one and group activities for the classroom or workshop
- Sample affirmations to increase feelings of self-worth
- A special listing of additional books on self-esteem
- And much more.

CANDACE SEMIGRAN is chief executive officer of Insight Seminars, an international private self-help organization with offices in over twenty-five cities— in the U.S. and abroad. She has been instrumental in developing an array of educational and self-improvement programs and has led workshops and seminars for thousands of people worldwide. She received the Who's Who in Professional and Executive Women 1987 Achievement Award and has twice received recognition from Who's Who in California. She is also the author of *250 Ways to Enhance Your Self-Esteem*.

Bantam Books of Related Interest:

TEACH ONLY LOVE
  Gerald G. Jampolsky, M.D.

LOVE IS LETTING GO OF FEAR
  Gerald G. Jampolsky, M.D.

LOVE IS THE ANSWER
  Gerald G. Jampolsky, M.D.
  with Diane Cirincione

THE POWER OF POSITIVE STUDENTS
  Dr. William Mitchell and Dr. Charles Paul Conn

HOW TO RAISE YOUR SELF-ESTEEM
  Nathaniel Branden

THE PSYCHOLOGY OF SELF-ESTEEM
  Nathaniel Branden

and on Bantam Audio Cassette

ONE-MINUTE SELF-ESTEEM:
CARING FOR YOURSELF AND OTHERS
  Candace Semigran

ONE-MINUTE
SELF-ESTEEM:

CARING FOR
YOURSELF
AND OTHERS

Candace Semigran

BANTAM BOOKS

NEW YORK · TORONTO · LONDON · SYDNEY · AUCKLAND

ONE-MINUTE SELF-ESTEEM:
CARING FOR YOURSELF AND OTHERS
A Bantam Book / October 1990

PRINTING HISTORY
Insight Publishing edition published 1988

ISBN 0-553-28561-0

Published simultaneously in the United States and Canada

Bantam Books are published by Bantam Books, a division of
Bantam Doubleday Dell Publishing Group, Inc. Its trademark,
consisting of the words "Bantam Books" and the portrayal of a
rooster, is Registered in U.S. Patent and Trademark Office and
in other countries. Marca Registrada. Bantam Books, 666 Fifth
Avenue, New York, New York 10103.

PRINTED IN THE UNITED STATES OF AMERICA

OPM   0 9 8 7 6 5 4 3 2 1

This book is dedicated to my dear friend, John-Roger, who has taught me more about loving and giving than anyone else I know—a man who demonstrates and lives what he teaches. Thank you for allowing me to work with you and with Insight Seminars. I am forever grateful for your presence in my life and for your unconditional love, support, and inspiration. I know I am a far better person for having known you, and I also know that our world is a far better place because of you.

Contents

Acknowledgments   xi

Introduction   xiii

1 **The Beginning of the Journey**   1
   Discovering there must be more to life . . .
   Wanting to be loved . . . Meeting a teacher

2 **Be Careful What You Ask For—**
   You Just Might Get It!   13
   Seeking fulfillment in the outer world . . .
   Getting caught up in desire, greed, and lust

3 **When You Are Sick and Tired of Being**
   Sick and Tired, You'll Change.   23
   Letting go of fear . . . Letting go of guilt and
   resentment

4 **Accepting and Trusting Yourself**   37
   Taking charge . . . Listening to the inner
   voice . . . Standing in integrity

5 **Relaxing and Loving Yourself**   47
   Forgiving yourself . . . Loving yourself . . .
   Taking care of yourself

6 The Attitude of Gratitude   **63**
    The value of focusing on what you are
    grateful for . . . An exercise in abundance

7 Giving Is Receiving   **71**
    The blessings of giving . . . Joy and fulfillment
    . . . The cycle of how to create greater
    abundance . . . Service—its own reward

8 Asking for What You Want   **87**
    What do you truly want? . . . How can you
    get it? . . . Are you worthy?

9 Setting Yourself Up for Success   **101**
    Striving for excellence . . . Dreaming big . . .
    Cycles for completion

10 Where to From Here? Loving Is the
Answer.   **119**
    Making a difference in the world . . . Creating
    world peace . . . Loving, caring, and sharing

Appendix A:
Exercises in Giving   **135**
    A list of anonymous ways you can give, serve
    others, and increase your self-esteem

Appendix B:
Affirmations for Positive Self-Esteem   **139**
    Sample affirmations you can use to increase
    your feelings of self-worth and positive
    self-esteem

Appendix C:
How to Fight the Blahs   **141**
    A list of things you can do to change your
    attitude and immediately start feeling better
    about yourself

Appendix D:
Workshops for Groups   **145**
THE GIVING AND RECEIVING WORKSHOP
SELF-ESTEEM EXERCISES
   One short workshop and a number of
   exercises to enhance self-esteem that can
   be done separately or together as a workshop
   for your class, your church group, a Girl
   Scout or Boy Scout troop, your employees, or
   any organization or group

Appendix E:
What Is Insight? Is There Something for Me?   **165**
   All about the Insight Seminar designed for
   individuals who want to enhance their personal
   or professional lives . . . A list of educational
   seminars for adults, children, teenagers, and
   companies

Appendix F:
Recommended Books and Tapes   **167**
   A list of books and tapes that are designed
   to enhance self-esteem, build self-confidence,
   and assist people in living happier, healthier,
   more abundant lives

My Gift to You   **171**
   A gift from my heart to yours

Acknowledgments

Special Thanks:

- to John-Roger for believing in me

- to John-Roger, Ken Meyer, Christopher Haupt, Russell Bishop, and my family for teaching me the perfect lessons I needed to learn

- to Rama Haggerty, Barbara Knight-Meyers, Patti Rayner, Katherine Boussarie, George Cappannelli, Annette Lawrence, and Dick Leight for encouraging me

- to Tom Boyer, Mary Ann Dickey, Terry Tillman, and the entire Insight staff for your friendship and support

- to Peter McWilliams and Rick Edelstein-Matisse for taking the time to read my manuscript and give me your feedback

- to Pauli Sanderson, Betsy Alexander, and Sandy Barnert for your editing assistance

- to Beth Hinman, Bruce Fox, Leigh Skinner-Fortson, Olga Messina, Stede Barber, Tom

Mondragon, and Mark Shoolery for your production assistance

- and to my wonderful husband, Stu, for all of your love, encouragement, and support and for sharing the journey with me.

Introduction

This book was inspired by my work with John-Roger and Insight Seminars, an organization that offers educational seminars designed to enhance people's personal and professional lifes.

I met John-Roger in 1963. These past 25 years have been the beginning of my journey—my journey into myself, discovering how to awaken the heartfelt energies and how to live, love, and laugh, learning how to be happy and how to know I am worthy, growing in my ability to love myself and others, learning how to create wonderful, successful, and nurturing relationships, and learning how to trust myself and communicate honestly and with confidence.

In this book, I share with you what I've learned in studying and working with John-Roger and Insight Seminars. I share with you techniques you can use to enhance your own self-esteem and boost your own self-confidence. Included throughout the book are exercises you can do yourself or with your family so that you can use the book as your own mini self-esteem workshop if you like.

In the appendixes I share with you

- Exercises in giving

- Affirmations for positive self-esteem

- Tips for how to fight the blahs

- Workshop formats you can use with groups to enhance self-esteem

I hope you enjoy your own journey into loving, caring, sharing, and positive self-esteem. If you find this book valuable and would like to continue your own process of self-discovery, I have included in the appendixes a list of books and tapes you might find of interest, information about how to obtain the workbook and audio cassette tapes that are designed to go hand in hand with this book, as well as information regarding the wonderful programs offered by Insight Seminars.

Enjoy!

CANDACE SEMIGRAN
August 1988

1

THE BEGINNING
OF
THE JOURNEY

1

The Beginning of the Journey

Once there was a little girl who was looking for love. She was a very smart girl, a good daughter, a bright student. She loved to learn, and she loved school.

She was also shy and afraid of making mistakes. She wanted things to be "perfect." So she worked hard to be a good student. She always did her homework, she studied a lot for tests, she turned in her work on time, and she received good grades. Because she loved to learn, she liked her teachers—or most of them. And because she received good grades, she sometimes was teased for being "teacher's pet."

At home she was the "perfect" child—at least in her parents' eyes. She would get up early each morning and practice the piano before school. After school she would take care of her younger brother. She loved her younger brother, and she didn't mind watching him after school. She felt like a little mother.

As she got a little older, her mother began working, and the girl took on more and more responsibility. She knew she needed to be strong. And she continued to try to be perfect.

When her father would come home and give her his paycheck, she would pay the family's bills. While her mother worked, she would cook the meals, wash and iron the clothes, clean the house, do her homework, and practice the piano some more.

Her parents were always proud of her. They showed her off to their friends. She knew they loved her.

The little girl thought that she was loved because of all the things she did, so she kept trying to do more and to do them better. She kept striving for perfection.

Sometimes she was a little jealous of her friends because they got to go on family vacations and travel around the world, or they got to go to parties. But she told herself that she could play later. Now she needed to learn and study and take care of her family.

Her favorite times were going to church and playing the piano because, in both, she found a sense of inner peace and joy. She would sit in church and not really understand what the minister was saying, but she would listen to the music, look at the beauty around her, and feel good. One of her favorite things at church was sitting and looking at a beautiful white marble round table at the altar that was engraved in gold: CHILDREN OF LIGHT ARE WE. She wasn't sure what that meant either, but she liked it. She knew that someday she would understand what it meant and that it was special. At home she would sometimes escape her problems by sitting down at the piano for hours to practice and play her favorite songs. These were times she could fantasize anything and be happy and at peace. And she knew she also brought joy to others while she played.

Then one day it started. Her parents started drinking and fighting, and then her mother would fight with her brother. The girl didn't understand why. Why would people who love each other argue and fight? In history class at school, she read about war and, again, she couldn't understand why—why would people want to hurt one another?

The little girl had a lot of love inside of her, and she wanted to share it. She wanted to love and be loved. She wanted her family and the whole world to join in this special loving. Why couldn't everyone just live together in love, joy, and peace?

She didn't understand, and she wanted to. There didn't seem to be anyone around she could talk to about what she was really feeling, so she kept quiet—and judged herself when she wasn't perfect, pushed her feelings down, and kept trying to be strong.

A lot of people would look at her and remark about how smart and strong the little girl was and praise her for all of the things she did. But inside she was hurting. She knew there had to be more. She knew there must be someone who could teach her more about loving, someone else who knew that loving was the answer, someone who lived their life in love, joy, and peace and could help her learn how to be happier, teach her more about love, and teach her how to assist others to know, too.

Then he appeared. It was September 1963, her first day of high school. And as soon as she walked into her English class that day, she knew she had met her teacher.

And the journey began . . .

The first day of class, her teacher asked the students to take out a clean piece of paper. "The first thing we are going to do each day," he instructed, "is take ten minutes when you can write about whatever you are thinking and feeling. Whatever comes to mind, just write it down. No one is going to see it. In fact, I don't even want you to reread what you write. You don't need to spell correctly; you don't need to write in complete sentences. Just write whatever comes to mind without judging or trying to analyze it."

So she wrote and wrote and wrote, and as the girl wrote, she found she was writing about problems at home, about feelings about her parents, about wanting to be liked, about judging herself and her life—and tears began to flow. She casually tried to wipe them away so no one would notice. At the end of the ten minutes, the teacher asked the students to put down their pencils, and without reading anything on the page, tear up the paper into little pieces and throw it in the trash. Wanting to do right, the girl followed the teacher's instructions.

Every day the teacher started the class this way. The girl began to notice that every time she wrote about what was bothering her and tore it up and threw it away, she felt a little better. And some days, when she would write about problems, all of a sudden she'd also find herself writing about possible solutions, solutions she hadn't previously thought existed. So day by day, she started feeling a little better about herself. Then one day she heard this statement:

EVERY DAY IN EVERY WAY, I AM GETTING BETTER AND BETTER.

She liked that statement and found herself starting to repeat it to herself. It seemed like a positive thought. She did want to get better. Maybe by thinking about getting better, she *would* get better.

Then one day the teacher asked her to stay after class. She immediately wondered what she had done wrong. But the teacher just wanted to ask her if she was okay, if there was something wrong. He had noticed her crying as she did the automatic-writing exercise that day and wondered if there was anything wrong, if there was anything she would like to talk about.

Tears started rolling down the girl's face. Yes, there was something that was bothering her. Yes, she would like the teacher's help. But she was embarrassed that she hadn't been strong enough (or so she thought) to handle the problem herself. And she began to tell her teacher that it bothered her when her parents drank a lot and argued and fought. She didn't know what to do. She loved her parents, and she loved her little brother. She was too small to try to physically stop her parents from fighting. She wished everything could be perfect, and it wasn't. She wanted her parents to show their love for each other and for her and her brother.

The teacher then told her about the three magic words:

I LOVE YOU.

And he suggested that whenever she heard her parents start to argue, she silently repeat to herself the three magic words and see what happened. He also suggested that there was one other person who probably would love to hear those three magic words—and that was the girl herself. The teacher suggested that every morning when she woke up, she look in the mirror, into her own eyes, and repeat the three magic words. And anytime during the day when she was in front of a mirror or a window that reflected her image, she could pause for a moment and repeat the three magic words to herself—out loud if she was by herself or silently if there were other people around. Then in the evening before she went to bed, while she was brushing her teeth, she could once again look in the mirror and tell herself the three magic words.

She thought the teacher's ideas were silly, but he was her favorite teacher and she trusted him. So she decided to play with the three magic words and see what happened.

The next time her parents started to have a disagreement in front of the girl, she just sat there and silently repeated, "I LOVE YOU," "I LOVE YOU, MOMMY AND

*Every day in every way,
I am getting better and better.*

DADDY," "I LOVE YOU." The girl was amazed at the results. Not only did she feel calmer and better inside but she felt like she was doing something constructive, and it seemed like after a few minutes, the power of her loving did reach her parents—or maybe it was just a coincidence that their fighting stopped!

The little girl also started saying the three magic words to herself in a mirror. It was funny. The first several times she said it to herself, she felt awkward and strange, and there was a little voice inside that said, "No, you don't. You're not worthy." But the more she said it, the better she felt. So she decided to say "I LOVE YOU" more often.

Exercises From Chapter One That You Can Do Yourself

1. Automatic-writing:

Take ten minutes to an hour each day and write about whatever is on your mind—your thoughts, feelings, problems. Without trying to think about something to write, write whatever is present with you. Like the girl, don't worry about spelling or complete sentences or grammar, and don't reread what you write. At the end of the time that you set aside for this process, tear up the paper without rereading it. Then you can either throw it in the trash or, if you have a fireplace, burn it. Then start noticing how you feel. I like to think of this process as "emptying out the garbage."

2. Affirming the positive:

**EVERY DAY IN EVERY WAY,
I AM GETTING BETTER AND BETTER.**

Spend a few minutes each day (or as often as you like) saying over and over to yourself the above statement. You can write it or say it to yourself in a mirror. Say it at least ten times each time you do it.

3. The three magic words:

I LOVE YOU.

As the girl did, play with the three magic words. You can say them to yourself as many times each day as you like. I suggest that you do this while looking at yourself in a mirror. Again, at first, as the girl discovered, you may have a little inner voice reply that it's not true. But I recommend that you keep doing the process. Over time, I think you'll find there are great results.

You may also want to play with the three magic words when you find yourself in situations where others are arguing or trying to make you or someone else wrong. I am not pretending this is a solution to everything, nor is it designed to replace taking action, but I certainly have found it useful over the years. Test it out for yourself, and see what happens.

2

BE CAREFUL WHAT YOU ASK FOR— YOU JUST MIGHT GET IT!

2

Be Careful What You Ask For— You Just Might Get It!

The girl had grown up and was now a young woman. She had completed high school and college, and she was now teaching school. Her life was very full. She had a job she loved, a new car, and wonderful friends. She was doing things in her life she had always wanted to do. But there seemed to be something missing.

So she decided to visit her teacher. She was scared. She hadn't seen him in a while, but she knew he seemed to be living his life the way she wanted to live hers. "I want to feel like I'm helping to make a difference in the world," she said to him. "I want to serve. I want to help people be happy. You seem to do that really well. Can I help you in your work?"

"Sure," he said. "There are always things to do. Go on in the other room. There is some work going on there where you can assist. They're expecting you. I told them you were coming."

"How did he know that's what I was going to say?" she thought. "Oh, well, who cares? He knew and I'm here and I'm getting to serve. That's all that matters."

So for several years, she worked closely with her teacher, who had also become her friend, assisting and serving hundreds of people. She loved her work. She loved knowing that she was helping people be happier and that she was making a difference.

But then she became dissatisfied. There still seemed to be something missing. Marriage, perhaps? "I want to love and be loved, be taken care of, and have more fun. Marriage is about giving and loving. Is it okay if I get married?" she asked.

"Sure, it's okay with me," said her friend. "Is that what you want?"

"Yes," she said. "Because I think there's more that could make me happier." And within a few months, the young woman was married, and it seemed like all of her childhood fantasies were coming true. She married a lawyer. They had two cars—a Porsche and a BMW. They went to fancy restaurants. He bought her pretty clothes and took her on expensive vacations. He loved her and took care of her. And she was happy—for a while.

Gradually, she started getting caught up in the things that the world could give her. "How about a Mercedes instead of a BMW? I want more fancy clothes. Can't you give me more spending money? What do you mean, we don't have enough?" She became dissatisfied again. She had thought that by getting all of those outer things, she would be happier. But she wasn't.

So she called her friend and asked if they could talk. "What did I do wrong?" she asked. "I thought that getting married and having fancy cars and all the things that money can buy would make me happier. But I feel empty inside. My stomach feels like there's a hole there. It even hurts. Where did I go wrong?"

"You didn't go wrong," said her friend. "You are just getting to learn an important lesson. It's important to remember that you are responsible for what you put in motion and for becoming involved in what other people put in motion. You've allowed yourself to get caught up in greed and lust, and these things shut off your ability to be joyful. You might want to be careful of what you ask for, because you sometimes get it."

"Life is a game," he continued, "and you just got caught up in it and were letting it master you instead of you mastering it."

"What can I do now?" she asked.

"Go to a park or the beach or somewhere you can spend some quiet time with yourself, and ask yourself a few simple questions:

1. What does taking care of yourself mean to you?
2. What do you want?
3. What experience are you looking for?
4. How could you get it?

"Then come back and we'll talk."

So the young woman went off to think. "Taking care of myself. Well, it means a lot of things. Doing what I enjoy doing. Getting rest. Having fun. Going to movies. Buying nice clothes. Getting a facial and having a manicure. Going out to nice restaurants. Reading good books. Exercising.

"What do I want? A vacation in Hawaii. What experience am I looking for? Freedom, relaxation, peace. How could I get it? I guess there are a lot of ways I could experience freedom, relaxation, and peace. I could spend more time in nature, going for walks at the beach, at the park, in the country. I could spend more quiet time with myself at home. Instead of turning on the television, I could listen to my favorite music and read and meditate. I guess I went chasing after symbols like cars and money

*Be careful what you ask for—
you just might get it!*

and relationships, thinking they would fulfill me, when what I really wanted was the inner experience."

After a while she went back to her teacher and told him the list of ways she had come up with to take care of herself.

"Exercising and resting are taking care of your body," he said. "Reading good books is taking care of your mind. Playing with your friends and being in a loving relationship are taking care of your emotions. What does taking care of *yourself* mean?"

"Well, maybe I don't know who myself is," she replied. "Maybe I'd better find that out first."

"That might be a good idea," her teacher said. "When you learn how to take care of yourself, then you can really help take care of others. Did you find out what you want?" he asked.

"Yes. I thought I wanted a lot of things. But when I was really honest with myself, I realized that the most important thing I want is to love and be loved."

"It does seem to keep coming back to that, doesn't it?" her teacher replied.

"Is it really that simple?" she asked.

With his usual knowing smile, he asked, "What do you think?"

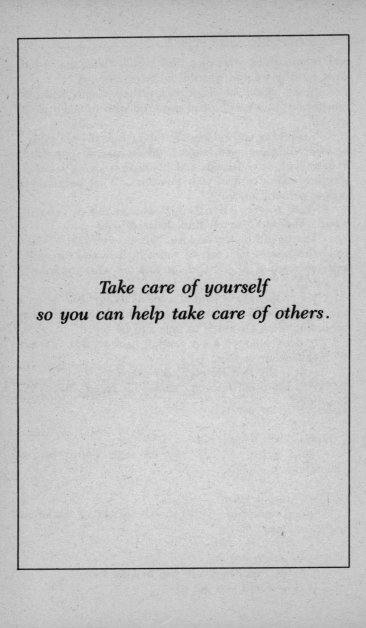

*Take care of yourself
so you can help take care of others.*

Exercises From Chapter Two That You Can Do Yourself

1. Quiet time:

Spend some quiet time someplace that makes you feel good and relaxed. It could be in nature, at the beach, in a park, listening to quiet, peaceful music—whatever helps you hear yourself.

2. Taking care of yourself:

Make a list of ways you can take better care of yourself.

3. What do you want:

Spend some time with yourself answering the following questions:

1) What do you want?
2) What experience are you looking for?
3) How could you get it?

3

WHEN YOU ARE SICK AND TIRED OF BEING SICK AND TIRED, YOU'LL CHANGE.

3

When You Are Sick and Tired of Being Sick and Tired, You'll Change.

Months went by. The young woman was very busy. The company she worked for was expanding rapidly, so she was working evenings and weekends to make sure things were handled well. She was doing a good job and was proud of her accomplishments.

But one day she realized that she had been working so much over the past several months that she hadn't taken any time off for herself—to nurture herself, play and have fun, or meditate and nurture her inner spirit—and those were parts of her life that were very important to her. She hadn't been taking any time to spend with her family or friends.

She was afraid—afraid to speak up at work and ask for an assistant, afraid she would be judged as not doing a good enough job, afraid of being rejected. She also felt guilty about not being able to get everything done in less time and, at the same time, resentful of some of her co-workers who left work at a reasonable time and spent weekends with their families. The few times she did take time off to go to a movie or spend time with friends, she felt guilty and that her boss would judge her and think she wasn't committed enough to her job or would get mad at her for being behind.

One day she felt so depressed that she started doubting whether she was even in the right career. She realized that she had been quite emotional now for days, crying without understanding why, having low energy, and feeling upset over the littlest of things. She finally decided to write her friend and teacher. Within two days she received a reply. He said, "Many years ago I taught you a technique of spending ten minutes to an hour a day writing to clear the mind and emotions, writing whatever thoughts or feelings are present and then tearing it up and throwing it away. What you are experiencing is the mental confusion and physical dis-ease that can result from letting all of that build up inside you. Oh well, when you get sick and tired of being sick and tired, perhaps you'll change."

The young woman then remembered the automatic-writing technique her teacher had taught her when she was in high school. So she went home to write. As she was getting out her paper and pen, she came across something she had heard her teacher say many times:

"IF IT WORKS FOR YOU, USE IT.
IF IT DOESN'T, HAVE THE WIT TO LET IT GO,
AND GO ON TO SOMETHING ELSE THAT DOES."

She realized that fear, guilt, and resentment were patterns that were no longer working for her. She wanted to let them go. She wanted to move on to something else that would work better for her.

So she sat at her dining room table for hours, writing, crying, tearing it up, throwing it away, and then writing some more. She felt a little embarrassed about crying but then realized no one was there to see her, so what did it matter? Besides, it was amazing how much better she was starting to feel.

Then she slept, and that night she had a dream. In the dream she saw a big sign that said:

> **The three greatest fears** = not being loved
> = being rejected
> = failure

In her dream she was walking down a path, and she came to a place where the road divided. One road led to LOVE, and the other road led to FEAR. Her teacher appeared at the intersection of the road and asked her, "Which do you choose? Love or fear?" And with that, the young woman awoke.

"I choose love," she heard herself saying as she awakened. "I choose love. But how do I let go of the fears? How do I let go of feeling guilty when I take time for me? How do I stop feeling resentment toward others? How do I give up what isn't love in order to experience more love? How do I forgive myself?"

The next day the young woman's teacher was giving a lecture at a local university, and she decided to drop in, visit her friend, and tell him about her dream.

The topic of his lecture that day was FEAR. "Fear," he was saying, "is all fantasy. Fear stands for

> **F**ANTASIZED
> **E**XPECTATIONS
> **A**PPEARING
> **R**EAL

"Most people fantasize. The question to ask yourself is, Do you want to win or lose in your own fantasy? If you want to lose, go ahead and expect the worst, doubt that you can succeed, visualize the situation not working out,

If it works for you, use it.
If it doesn't,
have the wit to let it go,
and go on to something else that does.

—John-Roger

and then let your fear stop you. If you want to win, expect the best, visualize the situation working out beautifully and successfully, just the way you want, and then move on that energy of success."

At the end of the class, the young woman approached her friend and thanked him for allowing her to sit in on his lecture. She told him about her dream and how perfectly his lecture related to what she was going through. Before she left, he handed her an envelope. Inside was a series of questions with a note that said, "If you'll spend some time with yourself answering these questions honestly, you can resolve some of your guilt and resentment and experience greater inner freedom. You might also want to spend some quiet time each day, sitting back with your eyes closed and reviewing the day. If there is anything you are judging yourself or others for, just say to yourself, 'I forgive myself for. . .' or 'I forgive _____ for . . . .' Forgiveness is simple. It's just a matter of doing it."

The young woman went home, took out her journal, and began answering the series of questions about guilt and resentment:

Guilt

1. *What do you judge about yourself?*
   I judge my body—that it's not a perfect "10."

2. *What do you tell yourself about that?*
   I tell myself that I'm not okay the way I am, that I am not beautiful, that I am not pretty, that I don't deserve to be beautiful, and that I will never be a "10."

3. *What "should" you do?*

I should stick to my diet and exercise program, lose weight, and look beautiful.

4. Is there anything you can do about that?
Yes. I can commit to myself and keep my agreements with myself. I can resume my diet and exercise program.

5. How can you resolve the judgment inside yourself?
I can forgive myself. I can realize that whatever I have done up until now has been the best I knew at the time. I can acknowledge my beauty as I am now. I can recognize that I can be my own worst enemy, and I can forgive myself for judging myself.

6. How can you be more loving?
I can love and accept myself the way I am. I can take the parts of my body that I have judged harshly and love them. I can start taking better care of myself and be gentler with myself.

7. Will you do that?
Yes.

I accept myself and love myself. My loving is the most important part of my behavior.

Resentment

1. What do you judge about others?
I judge others when they yell at people and treat them in an unloving way.

2. What do you tell yourself about them?

I tell myself that people who yell at others are wrong, that they are unloving and unkind.

3. What "should" they do?

They should be kind, loving, caring, and sensitive and should demonstrate their caring in all of their communications.

4. Is there anything you can do about that?

Either I can accept their behavior and love them anyway, or I can let them know that their behavior bothers me and that I'd like to see them treat people better.

5. How can you resolve the judgment inside yourself?

I can forgive them and realize they are probably doing the best they know how. I can realize that the standards of behavior that are right for me may not be right for others.

6. How can you be more loving?

I can love them for who they are and communicate my loving to them regardless of how they communicate with me. I can also do what I can to assist them.

7. Will you do that?

Yes.

I accept and love _____ (fill in their name). My loving for them is more important than their behavior.

And the young woman found that in her answers were some keys for her own forgiveness and freedom.

I accept and love myself.
My loving is the most important
part of my behavior.

Exercises From Chapter Three
That You Can Do Yourself

1. Automatic writing:
See page five in Chapter One for explanation.

2. Setting yourself up for success:
At a time when you can relax, take some time with your eyes closed to visualize a situation in your life where you've been afraid of failing. In your fantasy, see yourself succeeding. See yourself happy and smiling and everything working out perfectly. Feel what it's like to succeed. Hear the positive things people are saying to you; perhaps they are congratulating you on your success.

3. Forgiveness:
Take some quiet time to sit back with your eyes closed and review your day or week. If there is anything you have judged yourself for, you can say to yourself inwardly, "I forgive myself for _____ ," and fill in the blank. If there is anything you've judged another for, you can say to yourself inwardly, "I forgive _____ (fill in their name) for _____ ," and complete the sentence. It's amazing how taking just a few minutes to

complete and forgive can make a big difference in how you feel about yourself.

4. Guilt:

Take some time (using a journal, if you like) to answer the following questions. You can go through the questions as many times as you like.

1) What do you judge about yourself?
2) What do you tell yourself about that?
3) What "should" you do?
4) Is there anything you can do about that?
5) How can you resolve the judgment inside yourself?
6) How can you be more loving?
7) Will you do that?

5. Resentment:

As with the guilt questions, take some time with yourself to cycle through these questions as many times as you like.

1) What do you judge about others?
2) What do you tell yourself about them?
3) What "should" they do?
4) Is there anything you can do about that?
5) How can you resolve the judgment inside yourself?
6) How can you be more loving?
7) Will you do that?

6. Positive self-talk:

Write or repeat the following statements to yourself as many times and as often as you like:

I accept and love myself. My loving is the most important part of my behavior.

I accept and love _____ (fill in the blank with another person's name). My loving for them is more important than their behavior.

4

ACCEPTING AND TRUSTING YOURSELF

4

Accepting and Trusting Yourself

Several years went by. The young woman was busier than ever before. Her life was going okay. She was into a routine at work, and things were okay there, too. She did her part, she kept busy, and she was respected by her co-workers. People would go to her when they had something important to get done because they knew she would do it.

She was still working long hours—in fact, longer hours than before. It seemed that the more she did, the more that was given to her to do, and she would never consider saying no to anyone. She liked the acknowledgement she received for a job well-done, and she liked receiving approval from others, so she kept taking on more and more.

When someone told her how great a person she was, there was still a part of her that doubted it, but there was also a part that liked hearing it. The more she did, the more positive feedback she received, so she kept doing more and more and more, thinking that if other people felt she was good enough, maybe they were right.

A lot of changes had taken place in the woman's personal life. She had realized that her marriage was working neither for herself nor for her husband. She was making her work her first priority and spending 80 to 100 hours a week at the office, leaving very little time to give to a relationship. She realized it wasn't fair to her husband. He wanted someone there for him, and rightly so.

The woman struggled with this issue for quite some time. "Should I cut back at work and not give 100 percent and see if I can make the marriage work? Should I leave the relationship so I can dedicate all of my time to the business? Is it possible to do both things well?" She didn't know.

She finally decided that it just wasn't fair to her husband, and that she really wanted to give a lot to the business. So, after much discussion, she and her husband decided to separate. She decided that she would learn to take care of herself, that she could have a fulfilled life on her own, and that it was okay to be single.

Shortly after her separation, the woman traveled overseas to lead a seminar. At the seminar, she met a man who seemed so familiar. She knew she hadn't met him before, yet she knew him. And he seemed to know her. As they spent time together, the woman realized that this new friend was very special and that she had something to learn from him. Just being with him, she felt good. Looking into his eyes, she saw herself. She knew he loved her, and she loved him. She started to get a new picture of what loving was and what a friendship could be. She started to wonder, "Could a relationship be this good? This fulfilling?" This person loved her just for who she was. Somehow she knew that a romantic or marriage relationship with her new friend wasn't to be. Yet there was only one other person in the world she had ever experienced this deep a connection with, and that was her teacher.

During the course of their time together, she and her new friend both realized that the deep connection between them would always be there. It didn't matter that they lived on different continents and it didn't matter if they didn't see each other for years; there was a connection there that transcended time and space. So they decided to enjoy it and learn from each other.

When the woman returned home, she decided to take a seminar with some of her friends. During the course of the seminar, she got a very clear picture of herself always trying to prove she was okay, always trying to do things for other people, afraid to say no because she might be rejected, always trying to do more to prove she was worthy. It wasn't pleasant to look at, but she realized that she had never felt worthy for being just who she was, and that was why she had kept trying to prove herself through her accomplishments.

During one of her more difficult moments in the seminar, while she was seeing all of the things she had done in her life that hadn't worked for her, while she was reviewing all of the struggle and pain, from a place deep inside her heart she heard these words:

I AM WORTHY FOR WHO I AM, NOT FOR WHAT I DO.

I AM WORTHY OF LOVING AND BEING LOVED.

I AM ENOUGH.

The words resonated in her heart. She repeated them to herself, tears running down her face. She realized that she had spent most of her life trying to prove to herself that she was worthy of being loved. Because she hadn't felt worthy, she had been looking to others to tell her she was okay, and that is why she had spent so much time trying to please others and get their approval. It helped cover up the fact that she didn't feel okay about herself. She decided that from that moment on, she needed to take care of herself first. She needed to learn how to say no to people when they asked her to do something she didn't want to do or didn't have time to do. She needed to spend more time with herself. Most important, she needed to accept her worthiness and to be able to tell herself and *know* she was worthy, regardless of what anyone else might say or do.

She asked her teacher for his assistance and he gave her several suggestions. "First," he said, "I suggest you use that statement as an affirmation and repeat it often. 'I am worthy of loving and being loved.' Repeat it to yourself in the mirror. Write it a minimum of ten times a day in your journal. Write it on a card and post it in places where you will see it each day—on your bathroom mirror, in your wallet, on your desk, on the refrigerator. Say it to yourself as you wake up in the morning and again at night before you go to sleep. You've believed you weren't worthy for so many years, that it may take time to reprogram your belief system. So be patient with yourself and with the process. It takes time. And you're worth it."

After a month or two of using the positive affirmation, the woman returned to her teacher. "I can feel it starting to work inside, but I still have trouble trusting myself. There is still a part of me that doesn't believe in myself or trust what I say. Is there something you could suggest?"

"You may not like what I have to say," her teacher said. "There is one thing that, if you would do it, would produce greater self-confidence, greater self-esteem, and greater self-trust and would lead to greater self-approval, greater self-acknowledgment, greater self-respect, and greater self-worth. You would also have greater clarity, less confusion, and more energy, vitality, and aliveness."

"What is it?" the woman asked. "I'd like more of all of that!"

"It's simple," said her friend, "but not necessarily easy. Keep your agreements. Keep your word." He continued, "You say 'yes' to everything anyone asks you, and you think that will make them happy and keep approval coming your way. But you are setting yourself up for failure. You make so many commitments that there is no way you can keep them all. Some of them are in conflict. Some of them you forget. Some of them you decide are less important than others. Then when you break your word, you pay the automatic price for breaking your word: loss of self-trust, loss of self-esteem, loss of self-approval, loss of self-respect, loss of self-worth, lack of clarity, confusion, tiredness, and loss of trust by others."

"Do you have any keys for keeping agreements?" the woman asked.

"Yes," her friend replied. "Again, the keys are simple. But you will need to do whatever it takes to follow them:

- Make only the agreements you plan to keep.

- Write your agreements down.

- Make your agreements important.

- Renegotiate agreements when necessary.

"And remember: all of your agreements are with yourself, and some of them also involve other people. So when you tell yourself that you are going to get up at 6:00 a.m. and start your new exercise program or do your m̲ ̲ ̲ ̲tion, make sure that you keep your agreement with ̲ ̲

The woman started putting into practice t̲ had been given and found that she was star̲ herself more and feel better about herself.

Then one day, things started falling apart at work. There were some major financial problems, big enough that it might have become necessary for the company to close down, problems that the woman thought might have been prevented, had she been willing to risk speaking up. But she hadn't wanted to "rock the boat." She hadn't wanted anyone to get upset with her or think she was trying to take charge or pretend she knew everything. So to keep in their good grace, to keep the peace, and to keep approval coming her way, she had kept quiet.

After hearing about the problems at the office, she decided she had to take the risk. So she went to see her teacher. She told him the observations she had been making at work over the past few months, and explained that she hadn't spoken up for fear of being wrong. She told him what she would recommend and what she would do differently. She said honestly that she wasn't sure how to do it and that she was sure she would make mistakes along the way, but if he supported her, she would step forward, trust herself, stand up in her strength and integrity, and do her best to turn things around. She told her teacher she realized that she had to give up being liked by everyone, that some people would probably not like some of the decisions she would make, and that some people wouldn't support her. But the work that her company was doing was too important to her to let it end. And deep within her heart, she knew that it was time to start trusting her intuition, to start listening to that inner voice inside her heart and following its guidance.

A smile came across her teacher's face, and there was a sparkle in his eyes as he looked at his friend and said, "I've been waiting for you to step forward. I support you. Your plan sounds like a good one. Go ahead and see what you can do." So the woman started learning the value of trusting her heart in new ways.

*I am worthy of loving
and being loved.*

Exercises From Chapter Four
That You Can Do Yourself

1. Affirmations:

Use the affirmation "I am worthy of loving and being loved" or another positive affirmation you like. Take time each day to repeat it to yourself. You can do this looking in a mirror, relaxing with your eyes closed, or writing in a journal.

2. Agreements:

Set yourself up for success with your agreements. Make only the agreements you plan to keep. Write your agreements down. Make your agreements important. Renegotiate them when necessary.

3. Trusting your heart:

Spend some time each day listening to your heart. Learn to follow its guidance. Be honest. Have the courage to live in your integrity and to follow the truth as you know it, as a heartfelt response, with caring and consideration for others.

5

RELAXING AND LOVING YOURSELF

5

Relaxing and Loving Yourself

The next day as the woman was driving in her car, listening to the radio, she heard the song "Learning to Love Yourself Is the Greatest Love of All." She thought to herself, "That is my challenge and my next step—learning to love myself—but how?"

She came to visit her teacher just as he was beginning a class. She sat down in the back of the room and listened to his lecture. He was telling his class about a time he used to frequent a certain coffee shop and play the same tune over and over on the jukebox: "I Don't Care What They Say, I Won't Stay in a World Without Love." The topic of that day's lecture seemed to be that creating a world of loving begins by learning to love yourself. "Does he see me show up and do these lectures especially for me," she thought to herself, "or do other people go through the same kinds of things I do?"

As she observed that day's class, her teacher asked the students to choose partners. The partners were given 90 seconds each to brag about themselves, their lives, and

*Learning to love yourself
is the greatest love of all.*

—George Benson

their accomplishments. Then each received applause from their partner. She noticed that most of the students looked like they were having fun with this process; they were laughing, smiling, and excited to be bragging about themselves. Then she noticed a couple of students who reminded her of herself, who were crying and seemed to be having difficulty finding positive things to say about themselves.

After each partner had had an opportunity to brag, the teacher called the class members together and asked for their assistance. They formed two groups, each group sitting in a horseshoe or arc formation with an empty seat at the head of each arc. "The seats at the head of the arcs," the teacher explained, "are what we are going to call 'heart-seats,'" and into those two seats, he guided the two students who had been having difficulty.

The teacher explained that he would like the other students to start calling out all the positive qualities they had seen and experienced in the person in the heart-seat; all the person in the heart-seat was to do was to look in their friends' eyes and receive the positive feedback.

The woman watched as these two students seemed to transform before her eyes—learning that they were okay, learning how their friends saw so much beauty, strength, and courage in them, learning to receive the positive feedback. Tears rolled down the woman's face as she realized how hard she had been on herself, as she kept striving for perfection and falling short in her own eyes. She realized how much of her time had been spent in thinking, "I'm not okay," "I'm not enough," "I'm not good enough," "I'll never make it."

The teacher then continued his lecture, explaining to the class how energy follows thought. He wrote on the white-board:

> **As a man thinketh in his heart,**
> **So he becomes.**

"So," he said, "you might want to start observing the thoughts you hold in your minds. Are they positive ones or negative ones? Are they thoughts like 'I'm great! I can do it!' or thoughts like 'I can't. I'll never be able to. I'm not good enough'? My theory is that there is a part of you that listens to what you tell yourself and tries to follow your direction."

"Let's do a little experiment," he continued. "I'd like you to imagine for a moment that you have one day to enhance a friend's self-esteem. Make a list of things you could do, things you could say, gifts you could give them, actions you could take that would enhance your friend's self-esteem." When the students had completed their lists, the teacher asked them to look over their lists and circle any of the items on the list that they had given to themselves in the last two weeks.

"Someone once said that if we treated our friends the way we treat ourselves, we wouldn't have any! I want each of you to choose at least one thing on your list that you could do for yourself this week, and then commit to yourself that you'll do it. Then follow through and be a friend to yourself.

"That's the first part of your homework. And since we won't be meeting together again for a while, here are some things I'd like you to do sometime before our next class together:

1. Make a list of at least 50 positive qualities about yourself.

2. Sit down with your family or a group of close friends and do the process we did in class today, where one person sits in the heart-seat and the rest of the group calls out positive qualities and gives positive feedback about them. Make sure everyone in your family or group gets a turn in the heart-seat.

As a man thinketh in his heart,
So he becomes.

3. At least once a day between now and the next time we meet, take a few minutes to look in a mirror and say something positive to yourself, things like

"I LOVE YOU."

"I AM ENOUGH!"

"I'M GREAT!"

"WHAT'S BEAUTIFUL ABOUT ME IS _____ ,"

and fill in the blank.

4. Treat yourself as if you were your own best friend— because you are, you know. Treat yourself with kindness, caring, loving, and consideration. Take good care of yourself. I don't know if you realize it yet, but that is the most important thing you can do.

5. Each night before you go to bed, if there is anything that day that you have judged yourself for, just say to yourself (it doesn't have to be out loud),

"I FORGIVE MYSELF FOR _____ ,"

and fill in the blank.

6. Spend some time relaxing, perhaps listening to your favorite music. Take some quiet time with yourself.

After the students left, the woman went up to her friend and teacher and thanked him for the class. "I don't know how you do it," she told him, "but every time I come visit you, your lecture for the day is on the very

*Taking care of me
is the most important thing I can do.*

topic I am dealing with in my life! Thanks. I'll see you soon. I'm going to go get started on my homework!"

Over the next few months the woman practiced the lessons from that day's class. She started being more of a friend to herself. She started focusing more on her positive qualities. She again took time in front of the mirror to do her positive self-talk. At night before going to bed, she would review her day and forgive herself for anything she had judged about herself. She also started making more time to listen to her favorite music, to relax, to listen to meditation tapes and other uplifting tapes and read her favorite books. She spent more time going within, listening to her heart and looking for fulfillment there instead of looking to the outer world.

Almost as soon as the woman started discovering that she was enough, that she could take care of herself, that she was worthy, and that she could be happy if she went through the rest of her life as a single woman, a wonderful, loving, beautiful man appeared in her life. He was also involved in education and service. He was also dedicated to making this world a better place. He also held a vision of loving, peace, and joy. Through their relationship, the woman started discovering that she truly was worthy of having it all. He taught her a lot about trusting and giving and receiving. He was a joyful and playful man and started teaching her how to play and have fun. The day he asked her to marry him was one of the happiest days of her life. She immediately said, "Yes!" She realized how grateful she was to be able to share her life with someone she loved so much, and for the first time in her life she knew she could find the way to balance everything and give 100 percent to her marriage and 100 percent to her life's work.

The day before they got married, they called her teacher to thank him for a wonderful surprise wedding gift. During the course of their conversation, they asked him if he had any advice for them in their marriage. "Yes,"

Loving

Loving is the ultimate key.
When love is really present,
and flowing in your communications,
all other things tend to fall in line.

You find that your inner intent
of goodness and graciousness starts
writing itself on your eyes and face.

Then you start transforming everyone
and everything around you.

You don't even have to say a word.
No one even has to know what's going
on, but everyone starts feeling better.

And your loving is the key.

—John-Roger

he replied. "Make every day your wedding day. Keep the romance alive. Recommit daily to the lov-*ing*, the car-*ing*, the giv-*ing*, the romanc-*ing*, the liv-*ing*, the grow-*ing*. Then, instead of being married, you will be marriage-*ing*."

"What great advice!" they said. "And what a wonderful way to start our life together."

Exercises From Chapter Five
That You Can Do Yourself

1. Bragging exercise:

Get together with a friend and do the bragging exercise, where you each take turns bragging about yourself, your life, and your accomplishments. Congratulate each other! Have fun!

2. Heart-seat exercise:

Sit down with your family or a group of friends in an arc or horseshoe formation with one person seated in the heart-seat at the head of the arc. Take a few minutes for the group to call out positive qualities, and give positive feedback about the person in the heart-seat. Take turns so everyone in your family or group gets a turn in the heart-seat.

3. Positive qualities:

Make a list of at least 50 positive qualities about yourself.

4. Be a friend to yourself:

Pretend you have one day to enhance a friend's self-esteem. Make a list of the things you could say to or do for them to enhance their self-esteem. Now review the list and see how many of those things you have done for yourself in the last week or two. Choose one or more of the things on your list and do them for yourself.

5. *Positive mirror talk:*

Stand in front of a mirror and say something positive to yourself as you look into your eyes, things like

"I LOVE YOU."

"I AM ENOUGH!"

"I'M GREAT!"

"WHAT'S BEAUTIFUL ABOUT ME IS _____ ,"

and fill in the blank.

You might want to spend anywhere from a few seconds to a few minutes each day doing this. Don't be surprised if, when you first start doing this, you hear a little inner voice saying things like, "No, you don't. That's not true. No, you aren't." Just keep it up. It takes a number of positives to counteract a negative. So practice, practice, practice.

6. *Self-forgiveness process:*

Each night before you go to bed, spend a few minutes reviewing your day. If there is anything you have judged yourself for, you can inwardly just say the words

"I FORGIVE MYSELF FOR _____ ,"

and fill in the blank.

7. *Relaxation time:*

Take some time to relax—listening to your favorite music, going for a walk, taking a bubble bath—whatever is relaxing to you.

6
THE ATTITUDE OF GRATITUDE

6

The Attitude of Gratitude

Over the next few years, the woman continued her friendship with her teacher. One day he called and invited her to accompany him and a group of students on a special trip to another country. This trip turned out to be her perfect next lesson. For about ten days, the woman traveled through a country where many people lived in the streets, some in grass huts, some without any roof over their heads. She saw children without food or clothing. She saw people who were ill and dying. She saw children begging for something to eat or some money to buy food. This was her first time really seeing people at such a level of poverty and need. She found herself wanting to help the people in any way she could.

Upon returning home, she realized how protected a life she had led. As her horizons expanded, she realized that there were people in her own country, in her own city, in fact, who were also in need.

She realized that, prior to this trip, she had been focusing on what she wanted that she didn't have. She came home focusing on all she had in her life for which to be grateful—all of her blessings—and her deep desire to serve and give to others in even greater ways.

She sat down with her journal and started making a list of all the people and things in her life for which she was grateful: her husband, her parents, her teacher, wonderful friends, her home, her family, her education, the fact that she had food and clothing and indoor plumbing and the comforts of a nice home, her health, the ability to assist and serve others, being able to do the work she so loved and give to others at the same time, living in a country where she was free, love, joy, sunsets, ocean breezes, rainbows, flowers, riding bicycles with her husband, music, her quiet time alone, God's presence in her life, the dedicated team of employees where she worked, watching the deer and squirrels in the country, bundling up in the snowy weather, the list continued on and on. The more she focused on the people and things for which she was grateful, the better she felt, and her eyes started tearing up as she realized, "I do have a wonderful life!"

That night she wrote a letter to her parents, thanking them for all they had given her, all they had done for her, for loving her, for encouraging her and taking care of her, for all of the little things she appreciated about them, for giving her the greatest gift they ever could give—her life.

The next day she stopped on her way to the office and bought flowers and little gift cards for all of her co-workers and wrote them notes letting them know how grateful she was for their presence in her life.

She realized that she had spent a lot of her life focusing on what she didn't have and on what she wanted and saw how that perspective came out of lack. The trip abroad had been a reference point for her, showing her how much abundance she already had in her life.

Soon after, she stopped by to visit her teacher and thank him for all she learned during their recent trip. His lecture that day: "The Attitude of Gratitude." The students were sitting in pairs doing a process about gratitude.

1. What are you grateful for?
2. Why are you grateful?
3. How could you create, promote, or allow more of that in your life?
4. Who or what could you acknowledge more fully?

After the lecture, the woman approached her teacher and used the questions from the exercise to express her gratitude. As she looked into her teacher's eyes, she said, "I am grateful for your presence in my life. I'm grateful because you teach me so much about loving, about caring, about being the best possible person I can be, about loving myself and reaching out to share with others. I am grateful because you demonstrate in your own life what you teach."

Her teacher asked her, "How could you create, promote or allow more of that in your life?"

The woman paused for a moment and then answered, "I could become a teacher like you are and share what you've taught me with others."

As he smiled, he asked, "Who or what could you acknowledge more fully?"

She looked into her teacher's eyes and joy started filling her heart. "You, for being the best teacher I ever had!"

"And . . . ?" said her teacher.

"Oh, yes. And I am grateful to me for being a great student!"

Exercises From Chapter Six
That You Can Do Yourself

1. "I am grateful" list:
Make a list of all of the people and things in your life for which you are grateful.

2. Letters to parents:
Whether or not your parents are still living, you can do this process. Write a letter to your parents, individually or together, and let them know all of the things you appreciate about them and the things, opportunities, and lessons they provided for you for which you are grateful. You can mail it if you like, or you can throw it away. If they are living, you might consider mailing it, or writing them another "gratitude letter" and mailing it. I imagine it would bring them great joy to receive it from you.

3. Gratitude process:
You can do this process with a partner as the students did in chapter six, or you can do it yourself using your journal. Answer the following questions. You may wish to go through the questions a number of times, focusing on various people and things for which you are grateful:

1) What are you grateful for?
2) Why are you grateful?
3) How could you create, promote, or allow more of that in your life?
4) Who or what could you acknowledge more fully?

4. Gratitude to friends:

You might want to send a letter, card, or note to one or more friends, letting them know what you appreciate about them or how grateful you are for their presence in your life. You might want to think of ways you could demonstrate that gratitude to them such as flowers, gifts, poems, lunch, or a surprise of some sort.

7

GIVING IS RECEIVING

7

Giving Is Receiving

A few weeks later, the company the woman worked with sponsored a seminar about service. Her friend and teacher was the guest speaker. The topic of his talk: Giving and Receiving. "There is an interesting phenomenon that takes place in Israel," he began, "where the Jordan River flows into the Sea of Galilee. The Sea of Galilee has people living around it; there are fish there and there is life there and the water is very sweet to drink.

"That water flows out the other side of the Sea of Galilee to the Dead Sea, and there it becomes brackish and foul. I tasted it. It was terrible. In fact, if you drank much of it you could die; it is that poisonous. The same water from the Jordan River feeds both these bodies of water. The Sea of Galilee takes from the river, but it also gives. The Dead Sea just takes. There is no giving.

"When we stop giving in the spirit of giving, in the mentality of giving, in the emotional sharing, in the physically lifting and supporting, then we become like the Dead Sea—brackish and foul. And people stay away. They'll

All you have shall some day be given;

Therefore, give now

that the season of giving

may be yours....

—Kahlil Gibran

go by us only when they're having an emergency, and then they'll go by rapidly to get to some other place. Generally, people go to where there is living water. And you should have people come by you because you're living water and living life."

Her teacher continued to explain that there is a cycle of giving and receiving that, when in balance, produces great abundance. He then asked the group what they thought were the keys for giving with an attitude of abundance, and they quickly came up with a list:

- Having an attitude of gratitude—giving for the joy of giving

- Using what I've been given and then passing it on to others

- Taking risks in my giving

- Tithing to my church or favorite service organization

- Stretching—going beyond what's comfortable

- Detaching—giving freely without attachment and not being attached to what I have; enjoying it, using it, sharing it, giving it away

- Opening my heart continually to see what other ways I can give of my time, my money, my abilities, my gifts, my loving, my service

"In order to complete this cycle and have abundance, you can't just give. You must also be open to receive. What do you think are the keys for receiving with an attitude of abundance?"

- Having an attitude of gratitude—being grateful for what I already have

- Knowing I am worthy to receive—that I deserve it

- Using positive affirmations—writing them, repeating them

- Visualizing—seeing myself receiving, using, and enjoying whatever it is that I want

- Asking for what I want

- Trusting that I am always taken care of in perfect ways

- Opening my heart continually to myself as well as receiving more of the loving, the joy, and the abundance that's in store for me

As the students shared their keys, the teacher drew the cycle of abundance on the board:

The students were then asked to choose a partner and do an exercise about giving. Before beginning the exercise, the teacher asked them to close their eyes. "Ask yourself, What is there that you could give to people that would have the value of love, compassion, joy, justice, mercy, truth? What is it that you could give that could make a difference in someone's life as well as your own? How about your heart? What would it be like if you were giving of your loving heart?

"Now open your eyes and one of you ask your partner these three questions:

*That which you give
is that which you receive*

—John-Roger

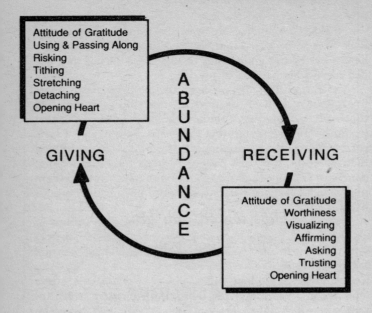

1) What can you give?
2) How can you give that?
3) What experience are you looking for?

_____

4) What can you give?

"You may have more than one answer to question #3.
When you seem to reach your bottom line for question
#3 and start coming up with the same answers, go on to
question #4 and then start over. After about five to ten
minutes, I'll have you switch so both of you have the
opportunity to answer the questions."

The woman joined the group in doing the process.
She realized that the greatest gift she could give anyone

was her loving, that the most important experience she was looking for in her life was experiencing loving, and that she would have both by trusting, by opening her heart, by risking and giving of that deep loving that she had always known was inside her.

At the end of the process, the partners were given five minutes each to ask for something they wanted that their partner could give them right there, something that would be nurturing and that they would enjoy, like a back rub, a foot massage, a shoulder massage. Or something that would be fun, like having their partner sing a song, dance, or tell jokes nonstop for five minutes. Or give them praise and tell them what a wonderful person they are for five minutes.

Then the seminar participants formed into groups of about 10 to 15 people each, and it was time for homework:

"The next process," the teacher explained, "won't take place in this room. In your groups, you will have the next hour to decide how you as a group would like to serve your community tomorrow morning. We won't begin tomorrow's seminar session until noon. You will have the morning to carry out your community service projects."

The sharing from the students the next afternoon moved the woman to tears—tears of joy and tears of gratitude for being part of a group of people so dedicated to loving and service. One group had visited a convalescent hospital, taking flowers and cookies and spending time talking and sharing with the people there. One group had taken a party with balloons and a clown to a hospital for terminally ill children. One group had spent time singing and dancing with a group of people in a convalescent hospital (one 100-year-old man played the piano as the group sang happy birthday to his friend who was turning 99 that day). One group said how much fun they had preparing breakfast at the beach for the homeless. Another group shared what an incredible experience they had painting a house for a family of seven and building some play equipment in the backyard for the children. And yet another group told of the joy they felt in spending their time giving anonymously to others through leaving change in phone booths for the next person making a call, putting money in parking meters so people wouldn't get tickets, and going into a restaurant and paying for a family's meal without their knowing who did it.

Several of the groups had received so much value from their service, had had so much fun and felt so good about what they had done, that they decided to make their volunteering a regular part of their lives.

When the teacher asked the group what they learned from this exercise, the group consensus was that in giving, they had received and that *they* were the ones who were truly served. One participant shared a quotation he had found that seemed to summarize their lesson:

> *My gift of giving is receiving.*
> *I reap what I sow.*
> *I sow generously, creatively, boldly,*
> *with an attitude of gratitude;*
> *my gift returns to me multiplied.*

> —Mark Victor Hansen, Ph.D.

At the end of the seminar, participants shared the various ways they planned to continue the cycle of giving:

- Cleaning out their closets and passing along those clothes they hadn't worn in at least a year

- Giving anonymously

- Volunteering on a regular basis at their church, at a school, hospital, or convalescent home, or with another service organization

At the end, they all made one request: that they come together again as a group on a regular basis to do group community service projects. And one of the participants offered to coordinate regular projects so that they all could join together in the spirit of loving service.

There are as many ways
to be of service
as there are to imagine.

Exercises From Chapter Seven That You Can Do Yourself

1. "How can you give" exercise:

You can do this process with a partner or by yourself, using your journal. Before you begin, close your eyes and ask yourself, What is there that you could give to people that would have the value of love, compassion, joy, justice, mercy, truth? What is it that you could give that could make a difference in someone else's life as well as your own? How about your heart? What would it be like if you were giving of your loving heart?

Then open your eyes and cycle through the first three questions below. You may have more than one answer to question #3, and that's fine. When you seem to reach your bottom line for question #3 and start coming up with the same answers, go on to question #4 and then start over. If you are doing this with a partner, you may take turns asking each other the questions. You may want to take about five to ten minutes each.

1) What can you give?
2) How can you give that?
3) What experience are you looking for?

---

4) What can you give?

2. Giving/receiving process:

This process is great to do with a partner, your spouse, your child, as a family, with a friend. Decide who is going to go first. That person will be Partner A. Partner A then asks Partner B for something that Partner B can give them within the next five minutes—a back rub, a foot massage, a shoulder massage, a song, a poem, a dance, a joke, a hug—something nurturing that Partner B could give them. If Partner B doesn't want to give Partner A what Partner A asks for, Partner A asks for something else. Partner B's job is to be honest. Partner A's job is to keep asking until they get a yes. Then take five minutes for Partner B to give to Partner A what they ask for. After five minutes, switch, and it is Partner B's turn to do the asking.

3. Giving community service:

Choose some way that you can be of service in your community. You might visit a convalescent or children's hospital and take flowers to a patient there, prepare a few sack lunches and give them to the homeless, or contact a local church and find out someone who needs assistance in your community (e.g., a house cleaned, a meal prepared, a room painted, etc.). For more ideas, see Appendix A.

4. Using and passing along:

Clean out your closet and pass along to a person, family, or service organization the clothes you haven't worn in the last year. Let others benefit from and use what you no longer need or use. It's amazing how, by cleaning out the old, you also make space for the new.

5. Anonymous giving:

Find a way to give to someone anonymously and notice how good it feels (e.g., leaving change in a phone booth for the next person, putting change in a parking meter, sending flowers, a card, or gift anonymously, buying a toy for a child anonymously). For additional ideas, see Appendix A.

6. *Volunteering:*

Select a local organization—your church group, school, educational organization, hospital, convalescent hospital, or service organization—and volunteer time on a regular basis (i.e., once a week or more). Just give and do whatever is needed, letting your service be your reward.

8

ASKING FOR WHAT
YOU WANT

8

Asking for What
You Want

The next time the woman visited her teacher, he was leading a discussion group on the topics of success, abundance, and creating what you want in life. As had always been the case in the past, this was the perfect timing for the woman to learn about these topics. "What keeps you from getting what you want in your life?" the teacher asked. "Money," one student replied. "Time," another one said. "I don't feel worthy of having it," another one responded. "I'm afraid to ask," said another. "Well, let's take a look at our belief systems," said the teacher. "If we have a desire to have a new car, a new home, and a lot of money and, at the same time, if we don't feel worthy of having it, are afraid to ask for what we want, or think we'll never be able to have it, I wonder what the end result will be. On one hand, we have a desire, and on the other, we have all of these beliefs. Are the beliefs supportive of having the desire, or in conflict?" the teacher asked.

"In conflict," someone replied.

You see things; and you say, "Why?"

But I dream things that never were:

and I say, "Why not?"

—George Bernard Shaw

"Are the beliefs positive and expansive, or are they negative and limiting?"

"Negative and limiting," another student replied.

"So, if we were to draw this scene, maybe it would look something like this:

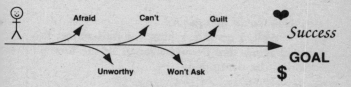

"In this scenario, do you think the person would reach their goal or not?"

"No," replied the class.

"So, what can people in this situation do to support themselves in reaching their goal?" the teacher asked.

The students suggested several solutions: "They could start focusing more on what they want than on the reasons or fears they have." "Yeah, they could expect the best instead of the worst." "They could do things to help themselves feel worthy to receive what they want." "They could ask a friend to brainstorm with them ways to get what they want." "They could also just practice asking for what they want."

"Lots of good ideas there," said the teacher. "Let's do a couple of exercises where you get to look at what you want and how you could get it. First of all, find a partner and sit facing each other. Do you remember when we looked at how you could give? Well, this process is going to work much like that one did. There are going to be three questions that you will cycle through a number of times. When you find yourself coming down to the same bottom line, the same response, in your answer for question #3, have your partner ask you question #4. Then start over. And after five to ten minutes, I'll have you switch so you both get a chance to play with this one."

1. *What do you want?*
   "I want to take a vacation with my husband," the young woman thought to herself.

2. *How could you get it?*
   "Well, I could ask him, I could contact the travel agent, and I could arrange for the time off work," she continued.

3. *What experience are you looking for?*
   "I want to have fun and spend time with my husband and relax."

Cycling through it again, she continued, making her answer to question #3 (above) her answer to question #1:

1. *What do you want?*
   "I want to have fun and spend time with my husband and relax."

2. *How could you get it?*
   "We could go for a picnic or bicycle ride."

3. *What experience are you looking for?*
   "Just to experience the loving and closeness with my husband."

As she continued to cycle through the questions, the young woman started coming down to the same bottom-line answer to question #3: "I want to love and be loved." At that point, she went on to answer question #4.

4. *How could you get it?*

"I could start by loving myself. I could reach out and show my loving more. And I could *ask* for the loving and for the hugs and cuddles rather than expect people to read my mind and know what I want."

"What did you learn so far?" the teacher asked the class. "A lot of what I want, I could get by giving it to myself or by asking others," one student said. "I learned I just haven't taken the time or had the courage to ask," another added.

"How many of you want things in your life that you don't ask for?" the teacher asked. Most of the hands went up. "So let's take this process a next step. As you answer this next set of questions, be sure to be really honest with yourself on #7. It is just fine for you to say no to that question. You may not be ready or willing at this time to ask for what you want, and that is okay."

1. What do you want that you don't ask for?

"A computer for our home," the woman thought.

2. Whom don't you ask? Be specific.

"My husband."

3. What is the fear?

"He'll think it costs too much and that I always spend too much money, and he'll say no."

4. What is the worst that could happen?

"He'll say no, get mad at me, and say he wants a divorce because I'm always spending too much."

5. What is the best that could happen?

"He'll say yes, we'll get the computer, and I'll write the book I've been talking about."

6. *What's likely to happen?*
    "He'll want to investigate prices and sit down and discuss it—and then he'll say yes."

7. *Will you ask for it?*
    "Yes."

8. *When?*
    "Tonight."

What the young woman learned that day was that she had a difficult time asking for what she wanted, fearing the worst and not feeling worthy, and that she had been affirming things not working out. She had told herself things like "I can't," "I'm not good enough," "They won't like me," "They'll say no which will prove I'm not worthy, so I won't ask. Then they won't say no, and I can pretend I'm good enough." She even had a difficult time picturing the positive, holding positive pictures in her mind of things turning out the way she wanted.

Yet, as she looked over her life, she saw that she usually got what she wanted and that most of the times when she asked, the answer was yes. She also realized that she needed to learn not to take a "no" answer against herself as a personal attack. "It keeps coming back to loving myself," she thought. "If I love myself enough, I'll accept what comes to me as being for my highest good, and if someone says no I can be grateful for that response as much as if they had said yes. Is it really that simple? I think so."

"Before we bring today's class to a close," her teacher was saying, "let's take a moment and look at what I'm going to call 'Intention and Method.'"

"If you wanted to travel from Los Angeles to New York, what are some of the methods you could use?"

"Plane." "Boat." "Train." "Walk."

"Which direction would you travel?"

"East," one student replied.

"Could you get there going west?" the teacher asked.

"Yes, but it would take you longer," replied the student.

"Okay, you start walking east and I'll take a jet west and who will get there first?" the teacher asked.

"Oh, I get it," replied one of the students. "There are lots of methods to get what you want."

"Yes," replied the teacher. "And I am going to suggest to you that if you have a clear and workable intention, you will find that there are a lot of methods that could be used to reach your goal."

"Next week our topic will be 'Setting Yourself Up for Success,' so we will be looking at this some more. In the meantime, let me give you your homework.

"What I'd like you to do before our next class is spend some more time going through the questions about asking and receiving—'What do you want that you don't ask for?' Also, practice asking for what you want. And I'd like you to make yourself a 'treasure map' of what you want in your life. Include physical things like cars, clothes, computers, etc., and also include experiences like loving, joy, giving, fun, what you'd like in your relationships, and the inner qualities you would like to have more of. You can take a piece of tag board and cut pictures out of magazines and glue them on the tag board. You can draw what you want. You can cut out words that represent what you want. You can include pictures of you or your own face. It can look like a collage if you want. Any way you want to do it is fine, and bring it to share at our next class."

The woman went home that night and asked her

Some things do not have to be said.

Some things are written
in the chambers of the heart.

Go within to read them; they're
there.

But you must have courage
to take the first step.

husband if he would make a treasure map with her. They cut out pictures of a new car, a ski trip they had been wanting to take, bicycles, some new furniture for their home, new dishes, a camera they had been wanting, a VCR, clothes, and pictures of couples together having fun, relaxing, playing, loving. They also included pictures of money, of people receiving a massage, of people working out and getting physically fit. They included words on their treasure map that described attitudes and states of being that were important to them—like *loving, light, integrity, dream, celebrate, joy, peace, winning, rich, happy*—and an abundance affirmation they had been using: "God is our unfailing supply and large sums of money come to us quickly under grace in perfect ways for the highest good."

As they glued the pictures and words on the tag board and created their treasure map, the woman realized that in addition to her unworthiness issue, she had also not wanted to focus on getting physical abundance and "things" in her life because she was afraid of getting caught up in greed or lust. She asked herself if she thought she was ready to be able to have all of the inner experiences like loving, peace, joy and fulfillment and also enjoy having more of the physical things in the world, like a new car, a vacation, more financial abundance and so on. The answer that came to her was, "As long as I keep focused on what is most important to me—and that is the loving, the caring, the giving, the joy, the peace, the service—if I put that first, yes, then it is okay for me to enjoy some of the other things, too."

That night, the young woman had another dream with her teacher. In her dream, he came to her and told her, "I'm not your father. I'm your friend. In the past you have asked me if it was okay to get married, to get divorced, to change jobs. Each major step in your life you have checked with me to see if I approved. I've noticed that in the past few months you have started trusting yourself more: with your recent marriage and with the way you are taking charge in your company. Have you noticed your own growth? If you haven't, take a look at the tremendous progress you have made. I am proud of you. And, yes, you are worthy of greater abundance in your life. You are such a giver. It's important to learn, also, how to receive."

Exercises From Chapter Eight
That You Can Do Yourself

1. "What do you want?" exercise:

Take time either using your journal or with a partner to cycle through the questions below. Each time, allow your answer to question #3 to become your answer to question #1 the next time you cycle through the questions. When you find yourself coming down to the same bottom line answer for #3 several times, go ahead and move on to question #4. If you are doing this with a partner, switch after about five to ten minutes, and you ask your partner the questions.

1) What do you want?
2) How could you get it?
3) What experience are you looking for?
_____
4) What do you want?

2. Giving/receiving/asking:

This process works similarly to the one above. You can do it either with a partner or using your journal. Be honest with question #7, and remember that it is okay to answer no. At this time you may not be ready or willing to ask for what you want, and that is just fine.

1) What do you want that you don't ask for?
2) Whom don't you ask? Be specific.
3) What is the fear?
4) What is the worst that could happen?
5) What is the best that could happen?
6) What's likely to happen?
7) Will you ask for it?
8) When?

Each time you answer yes to question #7, make yourself a note of what you agreed to ask for, whom you are going to ask, and when.

3. Treasure map:

Just like the class did, you can make yourself a treasure map of what you want to create in your life. Cut out or draw pictures of things you want (e.g., car, home, clothes, toys, money), of things you want to do (e.g., travel, vacation, play golf, jog, ski), and of words or pictures that represent qualities you want more of in your life (e.g., loving, joy, peace, sharing, giving). Glue them on a piece of colored tag board, creating a collage treasure map that represents what you want. Then put the treasure map up on a wall or somewhere where you can look at it often.

9

SETTING YOURSELF UP
FOR SUCCESS

9

Setting Yourself Up
For Success

The next time the woman saw her teacher was when she visited his class the day he was scheduled to talk about "Setting Yourself Up for Success." He had just drawn a diagram on the board and was beginning to talk about productivity:

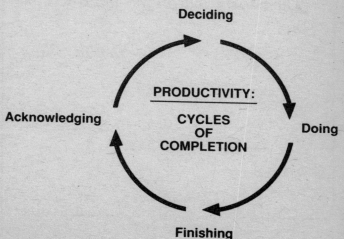

*People usually fail when they are
on the verge of success.*

*So give as much care to the end
as to the beginning;
Then there will be no failure.*

—Tao Te Ching

"In order to achieve and experience success in our lives, it is important to handle any unfinished business. Today we are going to take a look at managing our own productivity by identifying any areas of unfinished business and by looking at the implications of incompleteness.

"I am going to suggest that we define productivity as a cycle of action. A cycle of action has four steps:

1. **_Deciding_ to take action**

    You decide you want to do something. You decide to commit resources (time, money, people, equipment) to a specific project. Some people are great at starting things; others are reluctant to commit to taking action.

2. **_Doing_ the task**

    Some people seem to receive personal reward from working at a job rather than completing it. Some people start a lot of things, but because they fear failure or rejection, they appear to "get lost" in the doing stage and never quite complete the task.

3. **_Finishing_ the task**

    Taking the final step and completing a project or task is easy for some people and difficult for others.

4. **_Acknowledging_ yourself and any others involved in the completion of the task.**

    First, you want to acknowledge to yourself that the task is finished and that you are satisfied with the result. Second, you want to give acknowledgment to others and/or receive it. The person who completes the task wants to know that the result has been seen and the effort has been appreciated. Without acknowledgment, the person who performed the task may feel unappreciated and as though the task was without value. You may be the person who gives that acknowledgment or who wants to receive it from someone else.

"As you look at the productivity cycle, notice where you get stuck in the cycle. How many of you are great at starting things? How many of you sometimes appear to get lost in the doing and are afraid to finish something for fear it won't be good enough, someone won't like it, you won't be able to finish it, or you'll fail? How many of you find that finishing tasks is easy for you? How many of you remember to acknowledge yourselves and others or to ask for acknowledgment from others?

"If you can identify where you get stuck, you can then focus on strengthening those areas, and strengthening those areas where you have been consistently weak in the past can reap big results for you in your life."

Then the teacher wrote this on the board:

> *Small things done consistently*
> *in strategic places*
> *create major impact.*

"Let's do an exercise that will give you an opportunity to identify any incomplete actions in your life. Take out a piece of paper and start writing down anything you can think of that is incomplete for you: perhaps a project that is sitting on your desk, a paper for a class, a book you started but never finished, an item you borrowed from someone but haven't returned, a letter you said you'd write but haven't, someone you told you would call, a meeting you were going to set up, some equipment that needs repair, anything regarding your finances or banking, etc. Without analyzing anything or trying to prioritize, if it comes to mind, just jot it down.

"I am going to suggest that the incompletes in your life take a toll on your mind and body. What do you think are the results of having all of these incompletes in your life?

- Lower self-esteem
- Low self-trust
- Stress
- Tiredness
- Anxiety
- Confusion
- Lack of confidence
- Lack of trust from others

"There are other results that sometimes show up for people, things like lack of inspiration, alcohol or drug abuse, giving up, or feeling like a failure.

"Well, if you wanted to set yourself up for success, what do you suggest?"

"How about just completing things?" one student called out.

"Well," another said, "some of the things on my list are things I did finish but I forgot to acknowledge myself. I guess I could spend some time acknowledging myself and asking others to acknowledge me."

"What is something you did that you would like to be acknowledged for?" the teacher asked.

"I lost 25 pounds," the student replied.

"Okay, come up in front and, class, let's give him a standing ovation for his accomplishment."

"That felt good," the student told the class after they had stood and applauded him.

"How many of you would like to receive some acknowledgment?" the teacher asked. Almost everyone's hand went up. "Okay, get into groups of seven, and in your groups take turns sharing something that you completed for which you would like to be acknowledged. And the rest of you then give that person a standing ovation. Tell them how great they are, etc. Take turns until you have each had a turn."

Small things done consistently
in strategic places
create major impact.

When everyone had received some acknowledgment, the teacher asked the students to discuss ways they could support themselves in completing the things on their lists.

"I'm going to prioritize my list tonight," said one.

"I'm going to acknowledge myself for everything on my list that I've already finished and ask my family to acknowledge me, too," said another.

"I'm going to cross off my list the things I said I'd do years ago that I no longer want or plan to do and just declare them complete," added another student.

"I'm going to keep my list somewhere where I can see it often so I have a reminder, and then check things off as I complete them."

"All great ideas," replied the teacher. "What do you think your rewards or benefits will be if you keep better track of your incompletions and actually complete them?"

- Increased self-esteem
- Increased self-trust
- More energy to do more
- More relaxation

- Increased self-confidence
- Increased peace of mind
- Greater trust from others
- Greater inner peace

"If you want more of those benefits," continued the teacher, "then you might want to use some of the guidance you've just given yourselves about how to handle your incompletions." The teacher then went to the board and wrote:

$$S = \text{Sincerity}$$
$$U = \text{Understanding}$$
$$C = \text{Courage}$$
$$C = \text{Charity}$$
$$E = \text{Enthusiasm}$$
$$S = \text{Stability}$$
$$S = \text{Satisfaction}$$

"If you want to have more success in your life, here are seven keys. **Sincerity.** Be sincere in what you are doing, in where you are going, and in your communications with others. Be honest. Demonstrate integrity. Rather than forcing any of your ideas on others, set it up so you allow others to participate with you and allow them to experience success too.

"**Understanding.** Understand your task, project, or goal. Understand what you want, what you are after. Another way to say that is to be clear about your goal.

"**Courage.** *Courage* comes from a French word that means 'through the heart.' Once you have decided upon a goal and you understand it and are sincere in going for it, have the courage to do what it takes to reach your goal. Support yourself in completing it. And do it all with loving, through your heart.

"**Charity.** Share your success with others. Rather than being selfish, have charity for all people. Allow them to share in your abundance and success.

"**Enthusiasm.** Keep your enthusiasm before you as you move toward your goal. Keep the joy, the excitement, that bubbly inspirational energy alive inside of you, and let that energy help guide you to your goal. If something comes up as a block or barrier, or if you should fall down, let your enthusiasm pick you up and carry you forward. Do whatever it takes to get your energy to come alive and to get yourself back on the path, moving in the direction of your goal.

"**Stability.** Once you have said you are going to do something, do it. Follow through with it. This will produce stability as you move toward your success.

"**Satisfaction.** As you move toward your goal, do things in such a way that, when you reach your goal, you can feel satisfied. Create a result that allows you to say to yourself, 'I am a success' and feel it and mean it.

"Remember, too, that the thoughts you hold in your

mind are powerful. So hold positive thoughts. You may have heard this quotation from Henry Ford:

'*WHETHER YOU THINK YOU CAN OR YOU CAN'T, YOU ARE PROBABLY RIGHT.*' "

The woman realized that she had truly been her own worst enemy. Through believing she couldn't, she couldn't. Through feeling unworthy, she acted in an unworthy way and produced unworthiness around her. "Are my thoughts that powerful?" she thought to herself.

The teacher continued, "Your thoughts are very powerful. So hold positive thoughts in your mind. See yourself reaching your goal successfully and joyfully. Imagine what it will feel like to complete your goal and hear your friends acknowledging you and giving you a standing ovation."

"Is it okay to dream big?" asked one of the students.

"What do you think?" replied the teacher.

"Yes," the student whispered.

"What?" asked the teacher. "I can't hear you."

"Yes," the student responded.

The class quickly caught on to what the teacher was doing. "WHAT?" yelled the class. "We can't hear you?"

"YES!" shouted the student.

"Do you deserve success?" asked the teacher.

"YES!" replied the student.

"Are you worthy of having what you want?" asked the teacher.

"YES!" yelled the student.

"Okay," continued the teacher, "then here are two more keys to set yourself up for success. The first key is in one of my favorite sayings from Goethe:

'WHATEVER YOU CAN DO,
OR DREAM YOU CAN DO, BEGIN IT.

'BOLDNESS HAS GENIUS,
POWER AND MAGIC IN IT.
BEGIN IT NOW.'

"What's the key?" asked the teacher.

"Start. Begin. Get going. Doing. Take action," replied the class.

"You're right," replied the teacher. "Have I told you lately what a great and smart class you are?"

"And here's another key to set yourself up for success: remember that there is no such thing as perfection on this planet, so don't beat yourself up for not being perfect. Instead, strive for excellence. You can be excellent. You can do excellently. Excellence is within your reach!"

When the woman returned home that evening, she started reviewing the list of incompletions she had written down during the class. She then took her time management diary and copied the list into it, prioritizing the items as she went. She quickly realized that her two strongest areas were deciding/starting and doing. And her two weakest areas were finishing and acknowledging. "I wonder why those two are the weakest?" she asked herself. "Because you fear failure and rejection," she heard inside her head. "You are afraid people won't like what you do, so you don't complete it. You also don't think you deserve or are worthy of success or acknowledgment, so if you don't complete things, no one will ever know." "Someone inside there is pretty smart," she thought to herself. "Accurate, too!" she heard the reply.

"Okay," she thought to herself. "How can I support myself in completing more of the things I start?" First, she spent some time planning the rest of her week and the upcoming weeks and saw where she could devote some

*Whether you think you can
or you can't,
you are probably right*.

—Henry Ford

time to some of the items on her list. She also listed friends who could assist her with a few of her projects, friends who might have keys for her in taking the next steps. Then she went to her husband and told him about her day and asked him if he would acknowledge her for some of the things she had finished. She also spent some time acknowledging him for some of the things he had completed.

As she lay down to go to sleep that night, she spent some time reviewing her day, and acknowledging herself for the things she had done. Then she decided to take some time visualizing some of her dreams, feeling what it would be like to have completed them, getting her enthusiasm going, focusing on the courage, feeling worthy, preparing the way for greater abundance, success and the magic she knew would happen when she just put one foot in front of the other and took action—by taking the next step, and the next, and the next. "Big dreams start with little steps." She remembered what her mother used to say:

**"IT'S A CINCH BY THE INCH
AND HARD BY THE YARD."**

"I'll just accomplish all of my big dreams—an inch at a time!" And with that thought, she fell asleep.

Whatever you can do,
or dream you can do, begin it.
Boldness has genius,
power and magic in it.
Begin it now.

—Goethe

Exercises From Chapter Nine That You Can Do Yourself

1. Incompletions list:

Make a list of all of the things in your life that are incomplete. Projects you have started that you haven't finished. Books you have begun. Projects at work. Projects at home. The garage. The closet or drawers that need cleaning out. The equipment that is broken that you said you'd have fixed. The letters you said you'd write. The phone calls. The item you borrowed that you haven't returned. Cleaning out the refrigerator. Gardening. Handling your finances. Include anything that comes to mind.

Then, looking at the completion cycle, determine where you get stuck. Is it in the deciding and starting? In the doing? In the finishing? Or in acknowledging yourself or others?

As the class did, look at ways you could support yourself in completing the things on your list. Then one at a time, do it!

2. Acknowledgment:

Spend time with a friend or family member, asking for and giving and receiving acknowledgment for things you both have completed. Have fun with this! Let the acknowledgment in! You can also ask for a standing ovation!

3. Dreaming big—and taking it by the inch:

Take one of your big dreams. Write it down. Visualize yourself reaching it, doing everything it takes to complete it. Feel the success. Feel the satisfaction. See and hear inwardly your friends acknowledging you and giving you a standing ovation. Then open your eyes and break down your dream into do-able steps, remembering that it's a cinch by the inch. What is the next action step you could take toward your goal—and the next—and the next? List all of the actions that you are currently aware of and the people and resources that could support you in reaching your goal, your dream. Then plan out when you will take the next step. By what date? And when you have accomplished that step, acknowledge yourself. That way, you are acknowledging your way to success!

10

WHERE TO FROM HERE? LOVING IS THE ANSWER.

10

Where To From Here?
Loving Is the Answer.

One day, a couple of months later, the woman received a phone call from her teacher. "Hi. I'd like you to be the guest lecturer for my final class. It's next Tuesday, one o'clock. The topic is 'Where to from Here?'"

"But . . . what could I . . . ?" she started to ask.

"Listen to your heart. It knows the answer. See you there. Good-bye."

When the students arrived at their class the next Tuesday, the woman was already there. On the board she had written these words:

LOVING IS THE ANSWER.

LIVE YOUR LIFE AS A GIFT—
TO YOURSELF AND OTHERS.

"When your teacher asked me to talk to you today, the first thing that ran through my mind was, 'Do I have anything of value to share with these people that they don't already know?" Then I closed my eyes and focused on my heart, and I asked for whatever guidance was for the highest good. I asked, 'What would be of the greatest assistance to you as this particular class comes to a close and you all go your own ways and move on to your next steps?'

"Your teacher gave me a topic: 'Where to From Here?' As I was driving home from work that day, I heard a song by Louis Armstrong on the radio. The words I remember are, 'And I say to myself, what a wonderful world.' I started recalling some of the lessons my teacher had taught me, like the ground rules for living."

"The three ground rules?" one of the class members asked.

"Oh, you know them, do you?" replied the woman. "Why don't you review them for all of us?"

GROUND RULES FOR LIVING

1. **USE EVERYTHING FOR YOUR ADVANCEMENT.**

2. **TAKE CARE OF YOURSELF SO YOU CAN HELP TAKE CARE OF OTHERS.**

3. **DON'T HURT YOURSELF AND DON'T HURT OTHERS.**

"I see you've had a wonderful teacher," the woman said. "My life," she continued, "seems to be a journey, a journey of me discovering me, of me discovering loving, of me discovering peace, of me discovering joy, of me learning who I am. And I've discovered that whereas in the past I had thought there was a destination I needed to reach, I now know that life isn't about getting to a destination. Life is about enjoying the journey and learning and loving along the way.

"The answer for me to 'Where to from here?' is loving. Be loving. Live loving. Share loving. I used to get upset about wars and not understand why people and countries would fight. I wanted to know how I could help end war, how I could contribute to peace. I asked my teacher once about how I could help create more loving and peace in the world. His reply was so simple and so profound that I copied it down, and I carry it with me as a reminder:

> *'In awakening the heartfelt energies, you can't help but discover your own self-worth, your own self-love, your own magnificence. We really don't have the expression of outer loving until our inner loving is there. We aren't going to have outer peace in the world until we stop having the wars inside ourselves. That's our job—to start having peace inside.'*

"I know you have spent some time exploring the topics of success, abundance, and giving and receiving. As each of you prepares for your next steps, there is an exercise I think you might find useful. Why don't you each find a partner to work with, and then I'll explain what you'll be doing. There is a series of five questions, and you will each have about five to seven minutes to cycle through and answer them as your partner asks you the questions. I'll demonstrate it for you, using an example from my life. I suggest with this one that you cycle through, answering first from the personal perspective of your life. Then the second time through, answer from the perspective of what contribution you would like to make to the world. So I'll go through it twice."

1. *What contribution would you like to make to the world/your life?*

Ground Rules for Living

1. *Use everything for
   your advancement.*

2. *Take care of yourself
   so that you can help
   take care of others.*

3. *Don't hurt yourself
   and don't hurt others.*

The contribution I would like to make to my life is to take better care of my physical body. I've recently lost 30 pounds. I would like to lose another 30 pounds and get on a regular exercise program.

2. How can you do that? Be specific.

I could recommit to the eating program I did a few months ago for another six-week period, and I could set aside time at least five days a week to do my aerobics workout.

3. What risk(s) would it take?

It would involve a lot of discipline. I might have to give up certain things to make time for daily exercise. If someone invited me out for lunch or my husband and me over for dinner, I'd have to tell them what I was doing and ask for special foods. There would probably be times I'd have to tell people what I was doing and risk their disapproval if they had prepared a special meal, etc.

4. What inner qualities do you have to support you?

I am very strong. I do have a lot of discipline. I can be stubborn at times, and I could turn that into determination. I know how to persevere. I do have a lot of love for myself, and that will support me.

5. What is your next step? Be specific.

I commit to starting my program tomorrow. I will call the diet center today and let them know I am coming in to start again tomorrow. Then I won't chicken out because they'll be

*In awakening the heartfelt energies,
you can't help but discover your own
self-worth, your own self-love,
your own magnificence.*

*We really don't have the expression
of outer loving until our inner loving
is there.*

*We aren't going to have outer peace
in the world
until we stop having the wars inside
ourselves.*

*That's our job—
to start having peace inside . . .*

—John-Roger

expecting me. I will tell my husband tonight and ask for his support because his support assists me a lot. I will set my schedule for the coming week to be home in time to do my workout each day before dinner.

"Do you see how that works? Now, I'll go through a cycle in reference to what contribution I would like to make to the world."

1. *What contribution would you like to make to the world/your life?*

   I would like to help teach people how to love themselves and have more inner loving and inner peace so that we could start having more outer loving and outer peace.

2. *How can you do that? Be specific.*

   I could continue to facilitate seminars that assist people. I could write books that teach the keys to self-esteem, and I could develop a curriculum for schools in self-esteem and maybe even set up a model school where children are taught from the earliest years about loving, caring, sharing, and self-esteem. I hold a theory that if children are taught in this way, we won't have the current problems our nation is now facing with teen drop-outs, teen suicides, teen pregnancies, teen drug and alcohol abuse, and gang warfare. How can I do it? I can keep sharing my vision and theory with people until I find the people who want to help me make this vision a reality. I can also prioritize the ideas I just shared with you and take on one project at a time, one step at a time.

3. What risk(s) would it take?

Well, first of all, if I wrote a book, people might not like it. They might not buy it. It would take me risking people's disapproval. As far as developing a school curriculum and setting up a model school, it might take risking people thinking it can't be done or thinking I can't do it, and taking the risk of approaching people to finance the projects.

4. What inner qualities do you have to support you?

Oh, I have lots. I have loving, dedication, devotion, joy, enthusiasm, perseverance, compassion, empathy, determination. . . .

5. What is your next step? Be specific.

My next step is to write the book I've been talking about and get it published. The first step in that is to outline the book. And yes, I'll do that. I'll start tonight.

"So, go ahead and take about seven minutes each to cycle through those questions and see if you get some clarity for yourselves about your own next steps."

By the time the students had an opportunity to answer the questions for themselves, the time for that day's class was drawing to a close.

"Yesterday, I read a quotation from Ralph Waldo Emerson that appeared in a local newspaper. It seems so appropriate to our topic today. I'd like to share it with you:

'To laugh often and love much; to win the respect of intelligent persons and the affection of children; to earn the approbation of honest critics and to endure the betrayal of false friends; to appreciate beauty; to find the best in others; to give of one's self; to leave the world a bit better, whether by a healthy child, a garden patch, or a redeemed social condition; to have played and laughed with enthusiasm and sung with exultation; to know that even one life has breathed easier because you have lived—this is to have succeeded.'

"Each day, we are presented with many choices. Do we choose to be sad or happy? Do we choose to keep it to ourselves or to share what we have? Do we choose war or peace? Do we choose rejection or acceptance? Do we choose anger and resentment or forgiveness? Do we choose withdrawal or risking? Do we choose fear or loving?

"I have found that there isn't anything that enough loving won't handle. I suggest that loving is the answer. So love yourselves, love your friends, love the people you work with, even love your enemies. Take time each day to choose the loving. Thank you."

As the woman completed her talk, the entire class gave her a standing ovation. At the back of the room, sat her teacher, in the same seat in which she had sat when she came to visit. As the class thanked her, they asked her "Where and how did you learn all that you shared with us today? We found it really valuable." The woman glanced at the man sitting in the back row, smiled, and replied, "I have a great teacher!"

The End

(Or is it really the beginning?)

Exercises From Chapter Ten That You Can Do Yourself

1. Contribution exercise:

Take time either with a partner or using your journal to answer the following questions. I suggest you do it from both perspectives—how you would like to contribute to your personal life and to the world.

1) What contribution would you like to make to the world/your life?
2) How can you do that? Be specific.
3) What risk(s) would it take?
4) What inner qualities do you have to support you?
5) What is your next step? Be specific.
6) Will you do it? If so, when? And write it down for yourself in your diary, daily planner, or journal.

2. Choosing the loving:

Each day, take a few moments to rededicate yourself, to rechoose the loving in your life—inside yourself, in your relationships, at work. If you have a specific test or challenge (e.g., someone cuts in front of you on the highway), there's an opportunity to choose the loving. If someone tries to start an argument with you, there's a perfect opportunity to choose the loving.

APPENDIXES

Appendix A:
Exercises in Giving

Here is a list of ways you can give to and serve others anonymously and increase your self-esteem. Many of these ideas came from participants in Insight Service Seminars and The Confederation of Underground Philanthropists.

- Buy a little toy for a child and hide it in their room.

- Leave some change in a phone booth for the next person to find.

- Leave your waiter or waitress a thank-you card in addition to a tip.

- Fill up a parking meter, even when you are on foot.

- Go up to a person on the street, hand them a dollar, and say, "I think you dropped this," and walk away quickly.

- Pick up trash that is lying around your neighborhood.

- Say nice things about someone you dislike.

- Pay for the car(s) behind you in a toll booth. And then drive on.

- Have flowers sent anonymously to someone at work who works very hard but doesn't get much acknowledgment.

- At a market, give the checker $25 or $50 and say it's to be applied to the next person's bill anonymously.

- Drop some change in a public place, and leave it there for someone else to find.

- Send a thank-you card to a public servant.

- Leave a thank-you card on the windshield of a police officer's car.

- Leave small cloth bags filled with pennies in a schoolyard just before recess.

- Pay for a stranger's meal in a restaurant, without letting them know you did it.

- Anonymously pay a bill for a friend who might be having a hard time.

- Once a month, anonymously send a holiday card or gift to a friend.

- Ask your dentist, doctor, lawyer, or veterinarian if you can pay a bill for a client who might have trouble otherwise.

- Buy two theater tickets and give them to someone anonymously.

- Give without requiring a receipt.

- Get a group of friends together and do a job for a friend. While one of you gets your friend out of the house for a movie or something else, the rest of you paint their kitchen or do something else that they are needing to have done.

- Contact a local minister or service group and do a service project for a perfect stranger.

- Become a "guardian angel" for a friend, periodically throughout the year giving that friend gifts, cards, etc. anonymously.

- Send a present to one of society's servants—an IRS agent, a dentist, a politician, a teacher.

- Go out of your way to greet a former enemy with kindness.

- Clean out your closet and house and give away clothing, toys, etc. that you no longer need to the charity of your choice.

- Do the same with something you really like and still use.

- Drop some money into the shopping bag of a stranger at a grocery store; don't let the person see you.

- Prepare a meal for someone in need and have

someone else take it to them—from an anonymous friend.

- Buy a gift—something you've been wanting for yourself—and give it away.

- Arrange for a special treat to be delivered to someone you work with—to reward their good work—and do it anonymously.

- Send an anonymous gift to someone in a hospital or convalescent home.

Appendix B:
Affirmations For Positive Self-Esteem

I am worthy of loving and being loved.

I am loving and caring toward myself and others.

I am happy, healthy, and wealthy in all ways.

I am enjoying my relaxed freedom and heightened energy.

I am taking care of myself with joy and gratitude.

I am loving my healthy, trim, and well-toned body at my perfect weight.

I am bringing success, abundance, and upliftment to all involved in my professional interactions.

I am relaxed, calm, and at peace with myself.

I have all the resources, energy, and time that I need to be an effective person.

I am confidently interacting with people as I am serving, loving, and growing.

I am joyfully and easily creating all of the resources I need to do my life's work.

I am confidently giving of my overflowing love.

Large sums of money come to me quickly, under grace, for the highest good of all concerned.

I am joyfully trusting my heart as I am loving me and you.

I am comfortably receiving all of the money and resources I need to do my highest level of work.

I am lovable and capable just because I am me.

I am having fun!

I am learning quickly and easily.

I am a worthy, loving, radiant being, confidently expressing my love.

I am celebrating my life, creatively sharing my abundance.

Appendix C:
How to Fight the Blahs

- Count your blessings.

- See a funny movie or TV show.

- Read a joke book.

- Go for a long, brisk walk.

- Spend a weekend in a deluxe hotel and have breakfast in bed.

- Listen to beautiful music.

- Read a very good and engrossing novel.

- Exercise a lot.

- Rent a convertible and ride with the top down.

- Go to the airport and watch the planes land and take off.

- Buy a new, exciting game for your video machine.

- Look at old family albums.

- Sing songs around the piano with friends.

- Get a haircut.

- Go for a swim.

- Play with a dog or cat.

- Get some new tapes or records.

- Buy something you have always wanted.

- Fix up your house.

- Go to an art museum.

- Meditate.

- Clean out your closets or bureau drawers.

- List your assets and accomplishments.

- Call a special friend who always makes you feel happy.

- Take a long, warm, bubbly bath.

- Eat a large piece of chocolate cake.

- Hug a teddy bear.

- Buy yourself some beautiful flowers.

- Go for a walk in nature.

- Spend some time at a religious retreat.

- Go help someone in need.

- Visit a children's or convalescent hospital and spend some time assisting or visiting with those in need.

Appendix D:
Workshops For Groups

The Giving and Receiving Workshop

A one-day workshop for groups of up to 300 people. Chairs can initially be set up theater-style, although during the workshop, they need to be able to be moved from time to time. Music can be used at the discretion of the facilitator leading the workshop.

10:00 a.m. Welcome and Introduction

Facilitators introduce themselves, welcome group, and give brief overview of day.

Ground Rules For Today

1. Use everything for your advancement.
2. Take care of yourself so you can help take care of others.
3. Don't hurt yourself and don't hurt others.
4. Give and receive.
5. Have fun!

Move chairs to sides of room. Mingle, introducing yourself to one another (name, where from, why you are here today, what you would like to gain from today).

Exchange Process

Stop. Close your eyes. Think of something you have on your person that you consider very valuable. Take it and place it in your hands. Think of how you got it. Did you buy it for yourself? Was it a gift from someone? Consider what it means to you, what value you place on it.

Open your eyes. Find someone you would like to give a gift to. Face them, holding your precious object in your hands. Close your eyes and consider what it would be like to give it to them. What might it mean to them?

Stop and open your eyes. You won't be giving it away. How did that feel? What feelings came up as you considered giving it away? Any feelings of attachment? Scared? Joyful? Free? Etc.

Sit down with your partner and share what that was like for you, what feelings and insights you had, what you learned about yourself, etc.

Large Group Sharing

Points for facilitator to make during sharing:

• What were the limiting beliefs that showed up for you?

• What strengths do you have in giving?

• Giving and receiving is a cycle, it is in giving that you receive, etc.

• Letting go of attachment can create abundance.

• Attitude is a key.

- A gift can be found in every situation.

- As you give, you are given unto.

- What goes around comes around.

- What brings your limitations forward?

- What brings your strengths and giving forward?

11:00 a.m. Asking/Receiving Process
(Stack chairs at sides of room first)

Think of people with whom you feel incomplete in the giving/receiving cycle and what you would like to say to them. Walk up to different people and ask for what you want and/or deliver those important messages, pretending that the person you are talking to is one of the people with whom you feel incomplete. As you approach each person, call them by the name of the person you feel incomplete with. For example, "Mom, I want to tell you that you sometimes talk too much. Would you just give me a big hug without saying anything?" "Dad, I want you to know that you don't always have to buy me gifts or give me money to show me you love me. Would you just tell me you love me?"

This is a time for asking and receiving and for giving out of your loving. A time to be nurtured if that's where you feel incomplete.

After exercise: Get chairs and re-form theater style.

11:30 a.m. What Do You Want?

Some people go after physical things in life: They want more money, a better job, a relationship, a new house or car—and all of that is fine. Some people want more of the inner experiences, inner peace, joy, love. In this next process, you will choose a partner and face them, making eye contact. There will be a handout with a series of questions you will take turns asking each other. You will have about five minutes for one partner to answer the questions and then two minutes for the partner who has been asking the questions to give feedback. Then we'll switch and the other partner will have an opportunity to answer the questions. Start with whatever comes to mind that you want. Be honest with yourself and just see where this process takes you. When you are answering the questions and you find that you keep coming up with the same answer to question #3, go ahead and answer question #4, and then start over with #1.

Instructions: Find a partner and move your chairs so you are facing your partner. Hand out questions.

Before you begin, just close your eyes. Now take a moment and review this past year. Did you give to yourself all of the things that were necessary to make your life work so that you could give to others? Or did you deny yourself and make other things more important than you? A lot of the time, we make "things" more important than who we are. What is it you really want? And open your eyes, and you may begin.

1. What do you want?
2. How could you get it?
3. What experience are you looking for?

---

4. How could you get it?

Feedback for two minutes. Switch.

11:50 a.m. How Can You Give?

This will be a partnership process you can do with the

same person you just worked with. Again, there will be a series of questions. Again, when you seem to reach your bottom line for question #3 and start coming up with the same answer, start over. I'll let you know when it's been about five minutes and then your partner can give you feedback about what they heard you say. Then we'll switch, and it will be the other person's turn to answer the questions.

Before we begin, please close your eyes for a moment and ask yourself what you could give to people that would have the value of love, compassion, joy, justice, mercy, truth.

What is it that you could give that could make a difference in someone else's life? What could you give that could make a difference in your own life? How about your heart? What would it be like if you were giving of your loving heart?

You can open your eyes and begin.

1. What can you give?
2. How can you give that?
3. What experience are you looking for?

Feedback for two minutes. Switch.

12:15 p.m. Closed-Eye Process: Giving/Receiving

(This process can be done with dim lights and with some quiet meditative music playing in the background.)

Close your eyes, and just take in a deep breath. And as you let it out, allow yourself to relax. I'd like you now to imagine yourself in a beautiful place in nature . . . it can be anywhere. In a beautiful meadow, under a tree, near a bubbling brook, on the ocean shores, in a garden full of sweet-smelling, colorful flowers . . . wherever you'd like to be . . . somewhere in nature where you can relax . . . just find yourself there, enjoying the fragrance, the sounds, and how you feel.

In the distance you see walking toward you an incredible being. Your attention is drawn toward this bright light, and you realize that approaching you right now is your own master teacher or master consciousness. And they are bringing you a special gift.

As you receive the gift, you look at it, and you realize it represents the qualities that you have to give. Ask this special friend to assist you in examining the gifts that you have to give the world, your community, your family, and yourself. What is it that you want? What are the gifts you can receive from the world, from your community, from your family, and, from yourself?

What do you want to give? What risks would you have to take in order to give and receive those gifts? What is your next step? See yourself taking those steps . . . giving . . . receiving. Perhaps your master teacher or master consciousness will show you a symbol that could represent to you the keys for taking your next steps in giving and receiving. And if you want to, you can take a moment and ask this special friend anything else you would like to at this time.

And then thank them for the gift and for taking the time with you right now. Let them continue on their way and gradually, as you are ready, start bringing your awareness back to the present, to you in this room. Take in a deep breath, and let it out. You may want to stretch a bit and, as you are ready, you can open your eyes.

12:30 p.m. Sharing

Take a few minutes to share with your partner what you learned, what you want to give and receive.

Take another few minutes to give each other a short backrub.

Short large-group sharing: What you learned, what you want to give and receive.

1:00 p.m. Lunch Break with Giving/Receiving Process

Lunch assignment: During lunch, share your gifts with someone you didn't previously know and someone who is not in this workshop, and be open to receive in abundance. Give and receive. You can share your opinion, your loving, your money, your lunch. Somehow, have an experience of giving and receiving.

2:30 p.m. Group Sharing

What I learned about giving and receiving.

After a few minutes of taking sharing from the group, have everyone turn toward a neighbor and share about what they learned so that everyone gets an opportunity to share.

3:00 p.m. Gratitude Process

In this next process, we are going to explore the attitude of gratitude and how gratitude relates to abundance. You will be working with a partner as we have done earlier today. So please find someone you haven't yet worked with and would like to, and sit in your chairs facing each other.

1. What are you grateful for?
2. Why are you grateful?
3. How could you create, promote, or allow more of that in your life?
4. Who or what could you acknowledge more fully?

3:25 p.m. Gift Mingle

Move chairs along sides of room. Participants will mingle with one another, sharing, "I give you the gift of . . ." (e.g., my love, my support, my enthusiasm, my joy, etc.). After about seven minutes, stop the group and then have them continue sharing, "I accept from you the gift of . . ." (e.g., your joy, your laughter, your strength, etc.).

3:40 p.m. Closing Circle

Form one big standing circle in the room, holding hands with those on either side of you. Imagine that there is a huge heart in the middle of the circle. Start putting your love into the center of the heart. Start passing your love around the group . . . sending it out into the world . . . envisioning this gift of giving continuing to spread around the world. If you have a wish for the world, put that into the heart.

In closing, I want to acknowledge you for risking, for reaching out, for sharing your loving, and giving of yourselves today. And I encourage you, as you go out into your lives, into our world, to continue risking and reaching out and sharing and giving of your loving and allowing yourself to receive, for this is how we can all make a big difference in our world. Thank you.

4:00 p.m. End Workshop

Exercises In Self-Esteem

The following 12 processes are exercises in self-esteem that can be done with small or large groups. These exercises are samples of those used in the Insight Self-Esteem Workshop, Insight Graduate Seminar Series, and Insight Service Seminar. Several of the exercises can be put together to create a short workshop, or they can be used individually. You may want to instruct the participants to bring a journal or you could supply pens and notebooks. Most of the exercises here are appropriate for people of all ages, from children to adults. Enjoy!

1. "Bragging" Exercise

This process can be done in pairs or in small groups. The way I have outlined it below is for pairs and takes about five to ten minutes.

First hold a short discussion about bragging. How many people feel uncomfortable bragging about themselves? How many people judge others when they brag? How many people like to brag? In this next exercise, each of you is going to have the chance to brag about yourself, share all the great things about you as a person, about things you have done, and how wonderful you are. If you run out of things to say, you can repeat or make things up! Have fun!

Choose who wants to be partner A and who wants to be partner B. Partner A will go first.

Partner A brags about self for 90 seconds. Partner B then gives feedback about what they heard for 30 seconds.

Partner B brags about self for 90 seconds. Partner A then gives feedback about what they heard for 30 seconds.

Share how that was for you. You can write in your
journal for a few minutes about how that process was for
you and about the things you said, your bragging, what
you are proud of about yourself.

2. "Be a Friend to Yourself" Process

This process can be done as an introduction to self-
esteem and takes about 15 to 20 minutes.

Short discussion about what self-esteem means to
you.

Journal writing: You have one day to enhance a friend's
self-esteem. How could you treat them? What kind of
things would you do and/or say? Write a list in your journal.

Now go back and read over your list. How many of
those things have you done for yourself in the last two
weeks? Circle them on your list. Raise your hand if you
underlined more than half of the things on your list. Less
than half?

Someone once said that if we treated our friends the
way we treat ourselves, we wouldn't have any. I would
suggest that if you do more of those things on your list for
yourself, you will enhance your self-esteem. Be your own
best friend.

Choose something on your list that you want, can,
and will do for yourself this next week.

3. "Inner Beauty" Process

This process can be done in partners and is great for
small or large groups. The entire process takes approximately one hour.

In partners, share about the following:

When your friends give you positive feedback about
what they like, admire, or respect about you, what do
they most often tell you?

Closed-Eye Process

Close your eyes and think about those words that you just said. Which one or two are the core qualities that make up the essence of who you are? Using those qualities, complete the sentence, "My inner beauty is..."

Open your eyes. Share with your partner the sentence "My inner beauty is...." (After a few minutes, switch and have the other partner share.)

Group Milling Process

Stand up and move your chairs to the sides of the room. Walk around the room sharing with the people you meet, "My name is... and my inner beauty is...." (Let this process go on for a while to allow people to share with most of the people there. If you are working with a very large group, I'd suggest stopping the process after about 15 to 20 minutes.)

Closed-Eye Process

Close eyes. Get in touch with how you have sometimes hidden your inner beauty and how you could share it more fully. Imagine you are sitting in a field on a warm sunny day... it's a beautiful day with blue skies, ... a slight breeze... the field you are sitting in is like a green grassy carpet and feels so soft beneath you... you can smell and see the beautiful wildflowers around you... and off in the distance you see someone walking toward you. They look very friendly and wise, and they are carrying a gift wrapped in gold paper with a gold ribbon. As they approach you, they tell you that they have come to bring you a gift... that the gift is a symbol that represents your inner beauty and how you could share it more fully. So you accept the gift and open it, and it is beautiful... and you share with this wise person what the gift means to you... and you thank them for bringing you the gift.

And as they leave, you gently start bringing your

awareness back to the present, as you think about the gift and what it represents . . . what your inner beauty is and how you could share it more fully. . . and gradually, as you are ready, open your eyes.

Milling continues: And continue the milling, approaching each other, this time sharing, "My name is . . . my inner beauty is . . . and the way I could more fully express it is . . ." (Allow milling to continue for about 10 to 20 minutes, depending upon the size of the group.)

Sharing: Sit down together in small groups of about five and share how that process was for you and what you learned.

4. "What Do You Want?" Process

The following process is a great way for people to look at what they want in life that they are afraid to ask for. It is done in partners and takes approximately 30 minutes.

Form pairs. Decide who wants to be Partner A and go first and who wants to be Partner B and ask the questions first. Hand out the questions. Demonstrate how to do the process by going through and answering the questions once yourself. It's important to let the group know that it is okay to get to question #7 and say no because it is important not to agree to do anything they don't want to do. This is a self-discovery process for each person to see how they let their fears stop them and there may be some things that they are ready to ask for and some things they aren't—and it's all okay. There is no right or wrong here.

1. What do you want that you don't ask for?
2. Whom don't you ask? Be specific.
3. What is the fear?
4. What is the worst that could happen?
5. What is the best that could happen?
6. What is likely to happen?

7. Will you ask for it?
8. When?

Allow each partner to answer the questions for approximately 10 to 12 minutes, starting over with #1 after finishing with #8 and cycling through the questions again and again during their time to answer. Have the partner asking the questions write down what their partner agrees to do and when and give it to them when they are through answering.

When the process is completed, let the people share either in partners or in small or large groups how that was for them and what they learned.

5. "Car Wash" Process

This is a process for small or large groups. Have the group form two, four, or six lines (depending upon the size of the group). Have each pair of lines face each other. How long this process takes depends upon the size of the group.

First have a short discussion about what a car wash is. You can either lead into this process with each person thinking of themselves as their favorite brand new car, or you can lead into it by introducing this as the "human car wash," where each of us as we go through life may need from time to time some TLC to "wash ourselves off" so we "sparkle" once again.

The process works like this: One at a time, each person closes their eyes and walks through the car wash. Their only task is to trust and receive. As a person walks by, the people standing in the lines can massage their hands, their shoulders, their neck, their arms, whisper words of encouragement to them, tell them how great and wonderful they are—in other words, do or say something that would be nurturing, positive, giving.

Take time for each person to have an opportunity to go through the car wash.

6. "Words of Encouragement" Process

This exercise can be done with small or large groups. Have participants move the chairs to the sides of the room and come back to the center of the room standing across from a partner. Have each pair determine who is going to be Partner A and who is going to be Partner B.

Next do a short closed-eye process while everyone is standing:

Think of something in your life that you want to do that would be your next step . . . something that might involve a little bit of risking . . . something that you want to do but maybe have been putting off. If you did this "something," you would feel great about yourself.

Now bring to mind someone you love and respect. Imagine telling them this next step you want to take, and imagine just now what encouraging words or words of support they might say to you. And if those words of encouragement mean something to you, I imagine they might also be supportive of others.

In a moment I am going to ask all the Partner A's to open your eyes. Partner B's, your job is going to be just to stand there with your eyes closed and receive.

Partner A's, your job is going to be to walk up to anyone with their eyes closed. You can take them by the hand or put your hand on their shoulder and, using their name, whisper to them the words of encouragement you received. Then go up to someone else whose eyes are closed and, using their name, tell them your words of encouragement. And I'll let you know when it is time to stop. So Partner A's, go ahead and open your eyes and begin.

(After about 5 to 7 minutes) Okay, Partner A's, I'd like

you to finish up with the person you are with and then stop where you are and close your eyes. Just notice, Partner A's, how it was for you to give. And Partner B's, notice how it was for you to receive.

Now, Partner A's, it is going to be your turn to just stand there with your eyes closed and receive. And Partner B's, it is going to be your turn to walk up to anyone with their eyes closed and, using their name, whisper to them the words of encouragement you received in the closed-eye process. So go ahead and, Partner B's, you can begin.

(After about 5 to 7 minutes) Okay, Partner B's, I'd like you to finish up with the person you are with and then stop where you are and close your eyes. Just notice, Partner B's, how it was for you to give. And Partner A's, notice how it was for you to receive.

You can all open your eyes now, and why don't you form groups of four or five and share among yourselves how that process was for you—both giving and receiving.

7. "Strength Bombardment" Process

This process is excellent for groups of people who know each other or have worked together for at least several hours to a day or two so they have had some interaction with one another.

Have the participants form small circles of five to eight people (sitting in chairs is preferable, and this process can also be done on the floor).

Have each group sit in an arc with one person at the head of the arc in the "heart-seat."

Allow five minutes per person so that each person has five minutes to sit in the heart-seat. While one person is in the heart-seat, the rest of the group take turns telling that person what they perceive as the person's strengths (e.g., "You're strong, you're loving, you're caring, you're beautiful, you're a great friend, you're giving, etc."). An option with this exercise is to have one person be the "scribe" or "secretary" for the person in the heart-seat and record all of the positive feedback. Another option is to have the group give the person a "group hug" when they are finished delivering their feedback and before they go on to the next person in the group.

8. "I Am Grateful" Process

This is a process that can be done in pairs, in groups, or as homework individually or with families. It's very simple. Each person can make a list of the people and things in their lives for which they are grateful. If you are doing this in a group setting, you can have people share with a partner or in a small group. You can also follow the process with a discussion about the attitude of gratitude and mention that a great way to go through life is to take time each day to focus on what you are grateful for. When you start choosing everything in your life—and being grateful for it—it's amazing how you open yourself for even more good to come in.

9. Community Service Projects

This is a beautiful process to do in groups of 8 to 20 people. I have led this process with groups of up to 300 people, breaking the larger group down into smaller groups of about 20. I recommend that at least five to six hours be allowed for this process from the beginning planning stages to completion. Don't be surprised if many people want to do this one again and again. It's a great way to serve your community.

The way I have set this process up is to first have the participants break into groups of 8 to 10 (or with a larger group like 300, into groups of about 20). I usually start this process on a Friday or Saturday evening (the planning part) and let the groups carry out the projects the next morning. You can set it up whichever way works best for you.

First, let the groups know that they will have one hour to determine what and how they would like to do the next process, which will be deciding how and then working together to serve. They can visit people in hospitals, convalescent homes, or children's homes, for example. (I've had groups who decided to take balloons, flowers, food and create parties for the patients.) They can prepare breakfast for the homeless. They can clean up a park or beach. They can go to someone they know to be in need and clean and paint their home and do repairs. Whatever they want to do is fine as long as it is serving someone.

These are the ground rules I give the group:

1) Decide as a group and stay together as a group.
2) Stay in public places. Stay safe. Take care of yourselves, too.
3) Have fun!

Sometimes I have someone call local hospitals and homes in advance and prepare a list of places (with contacts and phone numbers) that are open to having visitors. Especially when I've done a workshop over a weekend, this has made it easier for the groups to do a project "overnight." If you have more time, the groups can make their own calls.

It's wonderful to set a meeting time and place for the groups to come together after the projects are completed, either for a meal or a party or to continue a workshop, so that they can share with one another what it was like for them. The learnings that take place with this process are magical. The rewards and gratitude are even more magical.

10. "Treasure Map" Process

This is a great process to do with people of all ages and is especially fitting when you are showing people how to focus more on what they want to create in their lives.

You can supply all of the necessary materials and do it as a group or have this project be homework for a class.

The project is to make a treasure map on some kind of chart or tag board, cutting pictures and words out of magazines, and pasting them on the chart. People can include their own pictures, too, and do drawings if they like. The idea is to make the entire treasure map a picture collage of what they want more of in their lives.

People can have a general focus of what they want more of in their lives, or the focus can be more specific (e.g., their ideal relationship, their career, their family, world peace, success, how they want to feel, etc.).

It's a fun project. I often ask the people to bring in their treasure maps to share with one another. Then I encourage people to tape them up on their walls in their homes so they can see them every day.

It's amazing—what we focus on, we tend to create. I have seen lots of people create vacations, jobs, cars, amazing results!

11. "Asking/Giving and Receiving" Process

This process works well in groups of three, can be done with people of all ages, and takes about 15 to 20 minutes. It's a great process for asking for what you want, giving to others, and allowing others to give to you.

The groups of threes can be sitting either on the floor or in chairs.

Have the groups decide who is going to be Partner A, Partner B, and Partner C (or Chocolate Cake, Strawberry Cheesecake, and Hot Fudge Sundae).

Partner A will be first. This person will first have three minutes to tell their two partners what they would like them to give away (e.g., "Partner B, I'd like you to go give three people a hug and then come back for further directions." "Partner C, I'd like you to go tell four people they look great today and then come back for further directions.") Other examples are telling jokes, singing songs, massaging shoulders, etc.

After three minutes, call time. And then for the next two minutes, Partner A gets to ask Partners B and C for anything that they want for themselves (e.g., a shoulder massage, foot massage, hug, etc.).

Then repeat the process with Partners B and then C taking the lead.

12. "Anonymous Giving" Process

One way to increase your self-esteem is to give to others without letting them know it was you who gave.

An exercise you can do with anonymous giving is to discuss the concept of giving and of giving anonymously. You may wish to read from the list in Appendix A entitled "Exercises in Giving." Then have people select some way they can give of themselves anonymously. You may wish to have them either write about their experience or share about it when the group is back together—what it was like, what they learned, how they felt, and so on.

Appendix E:
What Is Insight?
Is There Something for Me?

Insight Seminars is a division of the University of Santa Monica, with headquarters in Santa Monica, California.

Insight offers educational seminars and workshops to thousands of individuals annually in over 25 major cities in the United States and in England, France, Germany, Australia, Sweden, and South America.

Corporations, businesses of all sizes, educators and individuals from all walks of life have benefited from the Insight Seminar.

The seminars and workshops are designed to assist people in enhancing self-esteem, increasing personal effectiveness, and improving the quality of their personal and professional lives.

Some of the major topics covered in the seminars include:

- Hidden power: the dynamics of choice
- Inventing the future: what you want and how to get it
- Tools for relaxation and focus
- Unlocking your creative power
- Identifying skill and ability in yourself and in others

- Communication and feedback skills
- Deepening relationships with family, friends and co-workers
- Trust and openness: assessingrisks
- How to become assertive, appropriate and sensitive

Children's programs, teen seminars and self-esteem workshops are offered for the general public through Insight's Youth and Family Department. Through these dynamic programs, our youth are given the opportunity to work in nurturing environments with skilled facilitators on the themes and issues that assist them in their personal, social and academic development.

The ACE Program (Achievement and Commitment to Excellence) is addressing the need for positive self-esteem and lifeskills education in our nation's schools. Involving a comprehensive approach that includes training and support for teachers, students and families, ACE assists our youth in developing the self-confidence, positive attitudes, and awareness of personal and social responsibility that may well be the most important factors in their growth.

Corporate education programs presented by the Insight Consulting Group offer state-of-the-art programs to Fortune 500 companies, as well as small and mid-sized firms that desire tools and techniques for implementing high performance management, expanding productivity skills, increasing motivation, and reducing stress.

Free introductory information about any of the above programs may be obtained by contacting

INSIGHT SEMINARS
2101 Wilshire Boulevard
Santa Monica, CA 90403
(213) 829-9816
1 (800) 777-7750

Appendix F:
Recommended Books and Tapes

Books to Enhance Self-Esteem

YOU CAN'T AFFORD THE LUXURY OF
A NEGATIVE THOUGHT
John-Roger and Peter McWilliams.
Los Angeles, CA: Prelude Press, 1988.

WEALTH AND HIGHER CONSCIOUSNESS
John-Roger. Los Angeles, CA: Mandeville Press, 1988.

RELATIONSHIPS: THE ART OF MAKING LIFE WORK
John-Roger. Los Angeles, CA: Mandeville Press, 1986.

ONE MINUTE FOR MYSELF
Spencer Johnson, M.D. New York: Avon Books, 1985.

WHAT TO SAY WHEN YOU TALK TO YOURSELF
Shad Helmstetter. Scottsdale, AZ: Grindle Press, 1986.

RELEASE YOUR BRAKES
James Newman. New York: Warner, 1977.

THE PRECIOUS PRESENT
Spencer Johnson, M.D.
New York: Doubleday & Company, 1981.

TEACH ONLY LOVE
Gerald G. Jampolsky, M.D.
New York: Bantam Books, 1983.

LOVE IS LETTING GO OF FEAR
Gerald G. Jampolsky, M.D.
New York: Bantam Books, 1970.

TO GIVE IS TO RECEIVE: A Mini Course for Healing
Relationships and Bringing About Peace of Mind
Gerald G. Jampolsky, M.D.
Tiburon, CA: Mini Course, 1979.

YOUR CHILD'S SELF-ESTEEM
Dorothy Corkille Briggs. New York: Dolphin Books, 1975.

WAY OF THE PEACEFUL WARRIOR
Dan Millman. Tiburon, CA: H.J. Kramer, Inc., 1984.

THE ROAD LESS TRAVELED
M. Scott Peck, M.D. New York: Simon & Schuster, 1978.

THE POWER OF POSITIVE STUDENTS
Dr. William Mitchell and Dr. Charles Paul Conn.
New York: Bantam Books, 1986.

LOVE
Leo F. Buscaglia. New York: Ballantine Books, 1972.

LOVING EACH OTHER
Leo F. Buscaglia.
New York: Holt, Rinehart and Winston, 1984.

LIVING, LOVING AND LEARNING
Leo F. Buscaglia. New York: Ballantine Books, 1982.

LOVE, MEDICINE AND MIRACLES
Bernie S. Siegel, M.D. New York: Harper & Row, 1986.

HOW CAN I HELP?
Ram Dass and Paul Gorman.
New York: Alfred A. Knopf, 1987.

THE GIFT OF ACABAR
Og Mandino and Buddy Kaye.
New York: Bantam Books, 1978.

ILLUSIONS
Richard Bach. New York: Dell Publishing Co., 1977.

JONATHAN LIVINGSTON SEAGULL
Richard Bach. New York: Avon Books, 1973.

FEEL ALIVE WITH LOVE. HAVE A HEART TALK
Cliff Durfee. San Diego: Live, Love, Laugh, 1979.

MAKING THE BEST OF ME: A HANDBOOK FOR STUDENT EXCELLENCE AND SELF-ESTEEM
Stu Semigran and Sindy Wilkinson
Santa Monica, CA: Insight Publishing, 1989.

Music Tapes For Relaxation

MIRACLES: MUSIC OF THE SPIRIT FOR HARP, STRINGS AND WINDS
Rob Whitesides-Woo. Venice, CA, 1985.

SACRED JOURNEY
NOW Productions. Los Angeles, CA, 1980.

THE HEALER'S TOUCH
Max Highstein. Los Angeles, CA: Inner Directions, 1986.

GOLDEN VOYAGE
Bearns and Dexter. Culver City, CA:
Awakening Productions, 1978.

FRAGRANCES OF A DREAM
Daniel Kobialka and Andy Kulberg. Belmont, CA:
Li-Sen Enterprises, Inc., 1983.

PATH OF JOY
Daniel Kobialka and Andy Kulberg. Belmont, CA:
Li-Sen Enterprises, Inc., 1983.

FROM HEART TO CROWN
Rob Whitesides-Woo. Upland, CA, 1986.

FAIRY RING
Mike Rowland, Milwaukee, WI, 1982.

SOJOURN
Music of the Spirit for Piano and Orchestra.
Rob Whitesides-Woo and Scott Fitzgerald.
Upland, CA, 1986.

My Gift to You

Dear Reader,

Please accept this certificate as a gift from my heart to yours—as my way of supporting you in taking the next step in your personal development and enhancing your self-esteem.

In Loving,

Candace Semigran

Gift Certificate

This certificate entitles you to a $50 discount
for the Insight I Seminar or the
Insight Self-Esteem Workshop.
To find out how to register
and the dates and location
of the seminars nearest you, please contact:

Insight Seminars International Headquarters
2101 Wilshire Boulevard
Santa Monica, CA 90403

or call toll-free (800) 777-7750.

For further information regarding self-esteem audio cassette seminars and tape programs please write to:

> **THE INSIGHT STORE**
> 2101 Wilshire Boulevard
> Santa Monica, CA 90403
>
> **INSIGHT CATALOG SALES**
> (213) 453-0071

ABOUT THE AUTHOR

CANDACE SEMIGRAN is Chief Executive Officer of Insight Seminars, the Continuing Education Division of the University of Santa Monica. Insight Seminars is an international organization with headquarters located in Santa Monica, CA.

A graduate of LaVerne University (CA), Candace Semigran has received the Who's Who in Professional and Executive Women 1987 Achievement Award and has twice received recognition from Who's Who in California. In addition, she conducts seminars and workshops throughout the world. Currently she lives in Los Angeles with her husband.

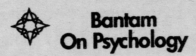

Bantam
On Psychology